THE INCREDIBLE
SHRINKING CHURCH

THE INCREDIBLE SHRINKING CHURCH

FRANK PAGE
with JOHN PERRY

B&H
PUBLISHING GROUP
Nashville, Tennessee

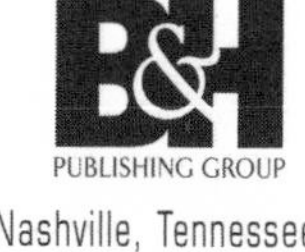

978-0-8054-4661-6

Published by B&H Publishing Group,
Nashville, Tennessee

Dewey Decimal Classification: 254.5
Subject Heading: CHURCH GROWTH \ CHANGE \
LEADERSHIP

1 2 3 4 5 6 7 8 9 10 12 11 10 09 08

I dedicate this book to my wife, Dayle,
and daughters, Melissa, Laura, and Allison,
for their constant and precious support.

Contents

Introduction

Today the church, like many traditional institutions in American, is under fire and struggling to prove its relevance in a postmodern culture. There's a whole stew of reasons for this that have been simmered and stirred together over the past generation and have been the subjects of countless books, research, commentary, and hand-wringing.

One component is the social and political upheavals of the 1960s—Vietnam protests, the mainstreaming of drug use, the sexual revolution, political assassinations, X-rated movies, and open challenges to traditions across the board. Antiestablishment rebellion took aim at structure and convention of every kind, including churches. Much of what church had traditionally symbolized suddenly seemed quaint and confining and irrelevant. As president of the Southern Baptist Convention, I have often stated that the issue of relevance must be attacked with the same passion with which we've fought the battle for rightness. I have often said that the early church was met with persecution, while the modern-day church is met with a yawn.

Another factor working against churches as an institution is the transformation of the American family. Half of all couples are divorced. Family members are scattered to the four winds. Everybody's working, even on weekends. When they're not at the office, they're working at home via Internet and cell phone. Lines between home and career are blurred and growing ever murkier. Even when people are home on Sunday, they're too exhausted to get out of bed in the morning.

Then there's the astonishing fact that in the last twenty years or so the First Amendment to the Constitution, which guarantees American citizens the right to worship freely, has been turned on its head and used to keep Christians from worshipping at all in the public square. I read somewhere that the phobia against Christianity has gotten so extreme that one Christmas recently the manager of a government-subsidized retirement home refused to let the elderly residents sing Christmas carols. Crosses and copies of the Ten Commandments that have been on display for decades are suddenly threats to the "separation of church and state." In today's culture that's a seriously misused and misunderstood phrase, which as you may know appears nowhere in the Constitution but came from a letter Thomas Jefferson wrote to the Baptists of Danbury, Connecticut, affirming that America would never have a state religion as Great Britain had, nor would Baptists be discriminated against under the Constitution as they had been under the colonial government.

I'll climb down off my soapbox in just a minute, but the point is that until the 1960s and '70s the American government supported and endorsed Christianity. The government and the church were allies; these days the government seems determined to crush any public expression of the Christian faith. Back in 1931, the Supreme Court declared in a ruling that as Americans "we are a Christian people." After Congress added the words "under God" to the Pledge of Allegiance in 1954, President Eisenhower commented enthusiastically, "From this day forward, the millions of our schoolchildren will daily proclaim in every city and town, every village and rural schoolhouse, the declaration of our nation and our people to the Almighty. . . . In this way we are reaffirming the transcendence of religious faith in America's heritage and future; in this way we shall constantly strengthen those spiritual weapons which forever will be our country's most powerful resource, in peace or war."

Yet eight years later the Court declared a public prayer unconstitutional because it was addressed to "Almighty God." A year after that, Bible reading in public schools was outlawed. By 1985 a moment of silence or voluntary prayer had been struck down by the Court as well. This was a complete repudiation of our founders' view of faith in general and Christianity in particular. Since 1620, when the Pilgrims landed in the New World with the stated purpose of planting their colony "for the glory of God and the advancement of the Christian faith," Christianity and American patriotism had been inseparable. Today Christian images in public places are being covered with tarps or chiseled away to dust by court order. So whereas church was once promoted and encouraged by governmental entities, now it's strictly hands-off.

The institutional church has taken some heavy flak in recent years, no doubt about it. But cultural trends and other outside forces aren't the true villain here. Yes, the world has not been a welcoming place for the traditional church lately, but those of us who love the Lord and see faith as essential to American life can't simply blame a hostile environment and let it go at that. These challenges give us no excuse for the fact that churches have in too many cases become lifeless, boring, and emotionally hollow. They have spiritually sputtered to the point where they have nothing left to offer. The rich, full, satisfying, supernatural power of Christ has dribbled away like air out of a punctured tire. People go through the motions of worship out of habit, but the internal fire has shrunk to a flicker. It's no wonder that church attendance is shrinking and congregations across the country are panicked over what to do about it.

Looking beyond our own crisis, we see this spiritual decline even more clearly in countries where religion has traditionally been controlled by the state, such as Great Britain, Italy, and Sweden. Taken for granted and run as a public bureaucracy, religion in these places makes no effort to identify or meet the needs of the people. No wonder that in Sweden, for example, only about 3 to 4 percent of the population attends church regularly. According to Eva Hamberg at Lund University, these "monopoly churches get lazy."[1]

Cultural shifts have affected the church, but they've also given it a historic opening. For one, morally conflicted and spiritually confused workaholics need Christ as much as their Pilgrim fathers did, if not more. We long for direction, long for assurance, long to know we mean something and that our lives are headed in the right direction. We've all heard about that "God-shaped hole" that nothing else can fill, and the best place to put God in your life is in church.

At a deeper level, we are made in God's image, and He desires a relationship with His people. As much as the world has changed since Thomas Jefferson's time, human nature hasn't changed at all. As challenging as it is for churches today to hang on, much less to grow and thrive, the same spiritual essence that produced vital and dynamic Christian congregations twenty years ago—or two hundred years ago—will produce them today. Energy, innovation, humility, research, leadership skills, and strategic risk-taking are all threads in the tapestry of church growth. But at the center of it is the faith that God will supply your needs as a family of Christ.

In Philippians 4:13 Paul writes, "I am able to do all things through [Christ] who strengthens me." Christ is the source of all success. But you can't just sit around and wait for Him to stop your church from shrinking. As I heard someone say once, you can't prove your faith by sitting on the railroad track and praying that the train won't come. There's a lot to learn and a lot to do in order to turn your church around, or to keep it headed in the right direction.

In Europe today young, enthusiastic, upstart evangelical churches are shaking up the old guard and reigniting a passion for everyday Christianity. Here in America, Protestant churches of every denomination, size, and style are bucking the trend toward declining attendance and bringing the gospel to God's people with new energy, new excitement, and a new, genuine sense of purpose. They achieve this by looking at challenges and opportunities from a fresh perspective and praying continually for God's blessing on their work.

No one set of rules will revive every church. Each congregation has its own history, baggage, opportunities, and tools. But healthy churches everywhere have attitudes and objectives in common. As a pastor who has led several shrinking churches to new eras of healthy expansion, it's my pleasure to share what I've learned with you here. This book is an expanded version of a presentation I've been invited to make many times titled "The Black Hole Baptist Church." I can reach only so many people per year traveling around with my PowerPoint setup whenever I can carve out the time. My prayer is that this book will give practical, actionable advice to pastors of all kinds of Bible-believing congregations to enable them to grow into the great kingdom churches God wants them to be.

The steps to success don't require big budgets, administrative geniuses, legendary preaching, or dazzling facilities (though any of these, properly and prayerfully managed, could surely be a big help). They are steps any church can take, which means that any church can be a healthy Spirit-filled one if its leaders and members will prayerfully and honestly dedicate themselves to the task. Wherever you are now in your growth cycle and whatever you've tried in the past, you can stop shrinking and start growing. Beginning now.

Stuck, Sunk, and Shrunk

Who zapped the church?

Like hapless characters in a B-grade science fiction movie, evangelical churches in America are going through an incredible shrinking act that defies every effort to stop it. Membership across the country is plateaued or declining. The church, its budget, and its influence in the community are shriveling, sometimes to microscopic size. Spiritually, far too many congregations have been transformed from all-powerful giants into little ants scurrying around the laboratory floor.

In most cases this hasn't happened all at once. It wasn't that one day all of a sudden everybody looked around and said, "Hey, this church is getting smaller!" or "Hold on! We're headed down the tubes!" It's been a gradual process. There was no big crisis or any major event that caused the church to change direction or accelerate the rate of decline. One year the church was growing, and the next year it wasn't. And by the time the members noticed, it wasn't clear how long there had been a problem or when it started. All they knew was that they were headed in the wrong direction.

Of course, a few members or leaders generally tend to be perfectly comfortable with things the way they are and put a high value on tradition and consistency even if it means other members and new member prospects drift away as a result. The percentage of members who feel this way varies from one church to another. However, if that percentage even approaches a tenth of the members, it can have a powerful negative influence on the body as a whole. But for the rest of us, growth is a sign of a healthy church, and stagnation or decline denotes a sick one.

If that's the case, American churches as a group are on life support. According to a special report published in *Leadership* magazine, of the approximately 400,000 congregations in the country, 340,000, or 85 percent, are either plateaued or declining in membership. Some are in crisis while others are soldiering bravely on, grateful not to be in worse shape than they are. These churches have lost their spiritual passion and become inwardly focused. They look toward the past instead of the future.

These incredible shrinking churches are the black holes of Christian evangelicalism. In case you've forgotten your high school astronomy, a black hole is an astronomical phenomenon that forms when a star stops shining, implodes upon itself, and collapses with such force that it has a density millions of times greater than Earth. Its gravity is so strong that it sucks planets and entire solar systems into it. Even light can't escape its gravitational pull, so astronomers see nothing but a black hole in the sky. They know the phenomenon is there by its effect on surrounding stars and planets they can see.

Shrinking churches have the same effect. They have ceased to become outwardly focused and passionate about their role in God's kingdom. They take on a defensive maintenance mentality, circling the wagons and forming a tighter and tighter spiral that pulls the spiritual life out of ministers and dedicated church members, and snuffs out any possibility of reaching the lost or nurturing new believers. Many church growth experts believe that one of the greatest impediments to a church's future is a glorious past. Members of these historic congregations tend to spend a great deal of time remembering the good ol' days and not thinking about the days ahead.

One of the most challenging and frustrating aspects of a shrinking church is that the more serious the situation is, the more scarce the tools for fixing it seem to be. Declining attendance leads to smaller budgets, which lead to reduced programs, which lead to waning enthusiasm and involvement, which lead to even lower attendance, still smaller budgets, and further emaciated programs.

And yet godly, well-meaning people sit paralyzed as their church gets smaller or respond to the pressure by drawing the inner circle of members and leaders even tighter. Author and consultant Tom Peters, who has written widely on the issue of organizational success, observes, "It is easier to kill an organization than it is to change it." Amen to that, especially when it comes to a church on a downward trend.

A Different World

I believe that if the 1950s ever come roaring back, thousands of American churches will be ready for them. The programs they hang onto so tenaciously were developed then and peaked in popularity when cars had big tailfins and gasoline cost a quarter a gallon. The fact that the world is an entirely different place now seems not to matter. They go on reaching out to *Leave It to Beaver* families—Dad works, Mom stays home (and vacuums in her pearls), the kids go to school, nobody's divorced or arrested or pregnant, and everybody's secure and content at the end of the day—despite the fact that the "traditional" family of working father, stay-at-home mom, and no divorces makes up less than 20 percent of today's population.

I'm not suggesting that the core message should change. The story of Jesus, His precious sacrifice, and His invitation to eternal life never change. But the tools and methods of proclaiming that story have got to change as the audience changes. Otherwise, from the outside looking in, the church seems irrelevant. Nobody cares. Yet the thought of changing it so that people *will* care is somehow frightening. We have a natural fear of abandoning the familiar.

And if we let go of what we know, what happens then? What do we grab onto?

Many churches are stuck like the church at Laodicia in the book of Revelation. The glory of God had departed from the participants there, and they had missed their opportunity to worship and draw close to Him. They were Ichabod churches, meaning churches that had lost their glory: their hearts had become so hardened that nothing would turn them from their eventual demise.

According to Revelation 3, the Laodician church had grown cold in its faith because the people convinced themselves they no longer needed God. They were successful by the world's standards, and they figured they could get along just fine without God telling them what to do. They were focused inward, concerned chiefly about their preferences and comforts. The Creator tells them in no uncertain terms that it doesn't work that way:

> I know your works, that you are neither cold nor hot. I wish that you were cold or hot. So, because you are lukewarm, and neither hot nor cold, I am going to vomit you out of My mouth. Because you say, "I'm rich; I have become wealthy, and need nothing," and you don't know that you are wretched, pitiful, poor, blind, and naked, I advise you to buy from Me gold refined in the fire so that you may be rich, and white clothes so that you may be dressed and your shameful nakedness not be exposed, and ointment to spread on your eyes so that you may see. (vv. 15–18)

The church probably still looked prosperous. It may have been a respected institution in the community. The members thought they were rolling along fine. But they had neglected their spiritual fire, and to God they were so revolting that He talks about vomiting them out of His mouth. Some translations have "spit" (the King James reads, "I will spue thee"), but the original Greek says "vomit," and I believe we have to face the unvarnished truth here: spiritually lukewarm churches make God sick to His stomach.

What's the cure for a tepid church with a room temperature faith? The presence of the Spirit of God in the hearts of its people! It gives them all they need to be rich and beautifully dressed and fully accepted in the Lord's eyes. God continues speaking: "As many as I love, I rebuke and discipline. So be committed and repent. Listen! I stand at the door and knock. If anyone hears My voice and opens the door, I will come in to him and have dinner with him, and he with Me. The victor: I will give him the right to sit with Me on My throne, just as I also won the victory and sat down with My Father on His throne" (vv. 19–21). A loving God chastens His people, but those who dedicate themselves faithfully and fully to Him share His victory over sin and death on the cross and His place with the High King of heaven.

It's Not Too Late

Can God restore your church? That depends. If you're too hard-headed and hard-hearted to change, you're probably zapped beyond repair. Sooner or later your church will collapse, and its light will go out just like a black hole. But if you're willing to look at your church differently, if you persevere, humbly seek God's face and will, and look forward with confidence, then yes, God can restore your church.

I've heard the argument that it's too late in America for a wholesale renewal in our Protestant churches. Naysayers point to statistics showing that the church in America is fast becoming like European congregations in their spiritual despondency and secular mind-set. The attendance figures are indeed shocking. For example, according to the British organization Christian Research, only 6.3 percent of the population in Great Britain goes to church at least once a week and this in a country where the government has traditionally supported a state religion and the queen is also head of the church.

There was a time when the Christian faith was alive in the British Isles and changing the world. Think of John and Charles Wesley, founders of the Methodist Church who led great spiritual revivals in the United States; John Knox, founder of the Presbyterian Church; and William Wilberforce, who almost single-handedly brought the slave trade to an end in the British Empire after a lifetime of effort. The great Baptist preacher Charles Spurgeon built the Metropolitan Tabernacle in London to hold the huge crowds that came to hear him speak every Sunday. Today the Tabernacle still stands and still has church services. But the huge six-thousand-seat interior looms over only three hundred or so worshippers on an average twenty-first-century Sabbath.

One widely quoted world survey finds that only about 4 percent of Swedes and 3 percent of Japanese attend church once a week or more. By comparison, a 2005 study from the Barna Research Group reported that 47 percent of Americans go to church weekly. However, it looks like the numbers have been slipping steadily over the past several decades, and younger Americans are less than half as likely to attend church as their parents' generation. An ABC News/ Beliefnet poll found that 60 percent of Americans sixty-five or older are regular churchgoers, compared with 28 percent for those age eighteen to thirty.

These are alarming trends. And they help explain why only 15 percent or so of the churches in America are growing and the rest are either shrinking or struggling to stay where they are. Odds are, then, that your church is in trouble.

But here's the good news: no matter what challenges you face in making your church a growing church, there's hope ahead. I've seen troubled, failing, seemingly hopeless churches transformed over a period of time into healthy, vibrant, growing organizations doing incredible work for the kingdom.

These churches have been both large and small, traditional and contemporary, and suffered from all sorts of problems in years past. Turning them around didn't take the same steps in every case, yet it took a focus on the same objective. The steps varied according to where the church was spiritually when the process began and what path it took to move to a higher level. But the goal was always the same: God-breathed spiritual renewal. Nothing else is possible without it.

A New Course

The church I pastor now, Taylors First Baptist Church in Taylors, South Carolina, near Greenville, has reversed course from a stagnant, struggling congregation to one that is on fire for Jesus. It had plateaued in 1993 and been slipping slowly and steadily downhill since 1997. Younger families were leaving over the church's lack of momentum and their dissatisfaction with a very traditional, performance-oriented worship style. What was done was done with quality. However, the narrow focus convinced many folks that the worship style would never be relevant to their twenty-first-century lives.

The church looked inward. While members wanted to reach out, they simply did not know how. To their credit, the church had developed a ministry to the sick and hurting unparalleled in any place I have ever seen before. For example, when a person went into the hospital, it set a mind-boggling chain of events into motion. Church staff called not only the patient's Sunday school teacher and deacon, but the care group leader, deacon, and Sunday school teacher of every family member as well. Sunday school classes, the Mercy Team, and other ministry groups swung into action in the case of sickness or bereavement. It was a wonderful ministry, yet it was sorely out of balance. Other aspects of Christian service were virtually ignored. For example, the church at large hadn't organized a mission trip since the 1970s.

When I arrived, one of the most obvious things to me was the need for updating the facilities and property. Ceiling tiles were literally falling on people's heads during Sunday school. Furnishings were tired and battered refugees from the 1950s and '60s. The recreation and youth facilities were antiquated metal buildings long past their prime. The sanctuary, constructed in 1995, was already showing wear and tear due to neglected maintenance.

As you might expect, these physical problems were symptoms of spiritual need: the evangelistic batteries at Taylors had run down. The former pastor had allowed the staff to function independently with little supervision or direction, resulting in a serious lack of cohesive vision. One of my first goals was to identify a clear vision for the future and give clear direction to the administrative team about how to achieve it. Some of the staff had been there thirty years and more. They were not too keen on having the new kid on the block come in and tell them how to do their jobs. Working with them was a challenge but ultimately a great success. They were able to retire with honor, and we were able to work together well until that retirement.

When we set out to turn Taylors First Baptist around, many people believed that the church's greatest days were behind her. They wanted change, yet as so often is the case, their battle cry was, "Pastor, I know we need change; just don't change what I like!"

We set about recommitting our church to Christ and His work. To serve Him well, we had to have proper facilities. We quickly moved to replace outdated buildings and update others. Out went the furniture and decorations of the Elvis era, and in came fresh, sturdy replacements that symbolized the fresh approach the church was taking to its mission. Along the way we made our buildings handicap accessible to ensure that everybody felt welcome.

More important, massive numbers of mission activities were added at every level. New staff came on to help with the increased outreach. Once these changes were in place, we as a church had a focused, cohesive vision again. Members and visitors alike responded to that vision. As a result, what was once an incredible shrinking church started to grow.

There was a huge change in mind-set and philosophy. A majority of the people in our fellowship have different and more passionate feelings about worship, evangelism, and missions today than ever before. Because of that, the church has dramatically increased its ability to reach out into the community and build a network of Christian fellowship. This change has had an incredible impact on our attendance, giving, and mission involvement. In four and a half years, we have seen more than a 130-percent increase in worship attendance and more than 70-percent growth in Sunday school. Our mission offerings have dramatically increased, and involvement with local, national, and international missions has skyrocketed.

God blessed me to be able to see this same thing happen in my last church, Warren Baptist Church in Augusta, Georgia. When I arrived, you walked in the door and suddenly it was 1957: same worship format, same furniture and accessories. Though in an area of tremendous growth, the church was not living up to its potential. Power struggles within various groups had left the church uncertain of its unity as a body and certainly uncertain of its future. On the corner of two major streets with access to every growing area in the county, the church simply did not know how to go beyond its own four walls. They needed vision and a patient but firm hand.

We tackled many of the same challenges I saw later at Taylors: run-down buildings, entrenched staff, and well-meaning Christians who were spiritually adrift. A vision was cast. Staff changes were made, some with great joy and others with more difficulty. Buildings were remodeled or replaced. In ten years there, I had the joy of seeing both Sunday worship and Sunday school attendance shoot up more than 300 percent. We became known as the church with the largest medical missions program in the Southern Baptist Convention. We saw many wonderful things happen, including dramatic increases in baptisms.

Problem? What Problem?

Before churches can even begin looking at a turnaround strategy, they have to admit there's a problem. Simple as it sounds, this turns out to be an impossible task for many congregations. Hundreds of them fall a little lower—or, in extreme cases, close their doors—

every year because they don't think there's anything wrong and don't take action until its too late.

In their book *Why Churches Die,* Mac Brunson and Ergun Caner point out the similarity between churches that are blind to the crisis situation around them and Samson, the Israelite judge endowed with legendary strength. The book of Judges tells of Samson's incredible accomplishments including tearing a lion apart with his bare hands and killing a thousand Philistines with the jawbone of a donkey. Then he fell in love with Delilah, whom the Philistine leaders bribed to find out the secret of his power. Delilah set to work using her feminine charms to get the information, but time after time Samson kept tricking her.

Finally she used the infamous demand, *If you* really *loved me, you'd tell me*: "'How can you say, "I love you,"' she told him, 'when your heart is not with me? This is the third time you have mocked me and not told me what makes your strength so great!' Because she nagged him day after day and pled with him until she wore him out, he told her the whole truth" (Judg. 16:15–17). That worked. Samson admitted that the secret to his strength was his long hair. "'If I am shaved, my strength will leave me, and I will become weak and be like any other man'" (v. 17).

While Samson slept, Delilah had his hair shaved off. Then he was captured by the Philistines, blinded, and bound in bronze shackles. Led into a temple to entertain a drunken bunch of leaders, he destroyed the building (his hair had started growing back) and killed his captors.

Samson "called out to the LORD: 'Lord GOD, please remember me. Strengthen me, God, just once more. With one act of vengeance, let me pay back the Philistines for my two eyes.' Samson took hold of the two middle pillars supporting the temple and leaned against them, one on his right hand and the other on his left. Samson said, 'Let me die with the Philistines.' He pushed with all his might, and the temple fell on all the leaders and all the people in it. And the dead he killed at his death were more than those he had killed in his life" (Judg. 16:28–30).

Brunson and Caner have an unorthodox but interesting take on this story:

> Though we often preach and teach otherwise, this was not an act of heroism; it was an act of desperation. Having seen the horrific results of a lifetime of bad choices and limited vision, Samson took himself out of the game. Notice that he did not even ask the Lord to defend the honor of his name or that of his children. Samson was selfish to the end. He asked for retribution on those who had taken his eyes. No spiritual reason. No honorable defense of the Lord who had called him. Samson was blind, suffering from advancing myopia to the end.[2]

Samson just rolled along through life ripping up lions and sleeping with prostitutes, not seeing the path he was on. His tunnel vision was hiding the danger of his decisions and actions from him, until it was too late. Churches roll along too, doing what they want to do, losing track of God's plan for them, and too often shrinking all the way to invisibility.

The Root of the Problem

New churches tend not to fall into this trap as often as older ones do. There's typically an evangelistic fervor to churches starting out that propels them along for several years or even decades. Of course every congregation has its own story, but all too frequently a staleness settles in to set the downward spiral in motion. Lewis A. Drummond pegs the general feeling exactly in his book *Ripe for Harvest*:

> After forty years of effective ministry, the church discovers that the original vision and mission that propelled the

> church forward have been forgotten. The plateauing of a church almost always involves increased bureaucracy, emphasis on maintenance, and unwillingness to change. Now the forms of ministry determine the function as organizational structures create needs rather than respond to needs. . . . Rigid structures prevent new ministries from being started and drive visionary leaders away to other churches.[3]

What a mess! Yet some churches recover from spiritual and numerical decline and go on to greater heights than ever before while others never start shrinking in the first place. In looking at specific causes of slow or no growth, it's easy to blame the challenges and distractions of contemporary culture for everything: We live in a secular society; families are scattered and rootless; music and television bombard us with hedonistic, self-serving messages; moral relativism has crept into our schools, governments, and other public institutions; and we're too busy scrambling around trying to keep up to think about church so it falls to the bottom of the priority list.

But the threat of becoming an incredible shrinking church isn't a recent phenomenon; modern times aren't responsible for so many churches being in trouble. The root of the problem has nothing to do with external pressures and everything to do with spiritual commitment. The apostle Paul saw churches around him struggle and sputter to survive, and yet neither he nor the church members ever heard a note of rap music or watched a single episode of *Desperate Housewives*.

Paul's Perspective

At first it may be hard to imagine how the incredible shrinking church of today could get any practical advice from the church in first-century Rome. On the surface the members' lives and experiences could hardly be more different: donkeys and campfires and clay flutes versus 747s and microwaves and iPods. But human nature really hasn't changed much in two thousand years. Despite the world of contrast in our everyday lives, the church then faced the same spiritual challenges it does now. The apostle Paul wrote to his young flock with advice about how to deal with all sorts of issues that came up among believers, issues that are familiar to anyone who's spent much time in church today. Paul's wise counsel, reaching across the centuries to us now, is as fresh and relevant as it was to those early followers of Christ.

That tiny network of first-century congregations was surely a prime candidate for being shrunken out of sight. There were only a few of them, with meager resources and no institutional traditions to draw on. They had to figure everything out as they went along. Paul had helped establish Christian churches across the Roman Empire, and now, writing from prison, he was advising the church at Philippi on how to solve problems and keep growing. If you want to keep your church from being zapped, take a look at the advice Paul gave to the Philippians.

A Joyful Mind-set

When Paul wrote his letter to the Christians at Philippi, they had been meeting for about ten years. The city was in the Roman province of Macedonia, in what is now south-central Greece, and Philippians were all granted Roman citizenship. Gold had been mined for centuries in the area, and more recently it had become a popular place for Roman soldiers to retire. Paul himself, along with his friend and coworker Silas, had set up the church there. At first it was a home church, meeting in the house of a hospitable Christian woman and successful cloth merchant named Lydia. By the time Paul wrote his letter around the middle of the first century AD, the Philippian church had grown to the point where it was meeting in a larger space. Paul didn't concentrate on physical trappings or size for size's sake. Yet over the course of his message, he touches on many of the core issues growth-challenged churches face today.

More than anything else, Paul's desire as a missionary had been to preach the gospel in Rome. If Paul could reach that city for Christ, it would mean reaching the whole Roman Empire. Though he had wanted to go to Rome as a preacher, he went as a prisoner instead. Most of us would consider this change of plans a failure but not this man. Paul had a joyful mind-set even in the midst of the toughest situations. He had faith that God knew better than he did what was best for His kingdom, and he went boldly wherever God called him. His happiness and contentment with the church in Philippi didn't come from big attendance figures or impressive church anniversary celebrations (though there's nothing wrong with either of those!). Paul found his joy in winning others to Jesus. In Philippians 1:10 he encourages the church to put aside petty issues "so that you can determine what really matters and can be pure and blameless in the day of Christ."

Turning to his own life as an example in verses 12–13, he declares that his imprisonment "has actually resulted in the advancement of the gospel, so that it has become known throughout the whole imperial guard, and to everyone else, that my imprisonment is for Christ." Paul wanted to make sure the Philippian Christians knew his arrest and imprisonment had not stopped the gospel's progress. Instead of hindering his preaching, prison bonds had extended it. Little did the Romans realize that the chains on Paul's wrists didn't bind his faith and his message but actually propelled them on their way.

Churches today need to remember that God has placed them where they are and that they can be used for His glory no matter what the circumstances: "He who started a good work in you will carry it on to completion until the day of Christ Jesus" (v. 6). Shrinking churches need a change of mind-set. They should realize that, despite the fact that their community is changing or their ministry needs total revamping, God has placed them where they are to be an encouragement to the saved as well as an outreach to the lost. Paul added that his term behind bars also gave encouragement to others who were preaching the gospel: "Most of the brothers in the Lord have gained confidence from my imprisonment and dare even more to speak the message fearlessly" (v. 14).

I believe God wants all our churches to see their current circumstance as an opportunity to do what Paul did, which is, to encourage fellow believers and at the same time reach out to the lost. That's part of Paul's message to us across the years through the Word of God. Do you have a joyful mind-set regardless of the condition your church is in? Until you do, your church is in trouble.

Whose Church Is It?

Another lesson Paul had for the Philippians that's still important and relevant today is that our motives in building our church have to be pure. If you're growing to the glory of God, He will bless your efforts. If you're growing to the glory of Main Street Baptist Church,

He's going to leave you to fend for yourself until you remember that it's His church and not yours. Beginning in Philippians 1:15, Paul wrote, "Some, to be sure, preach Christ out of envy and strife. . . . Others proclaim Christ out of rivalry, not sincerely" (15, 17). It's hard to believe that anyone in the church would act this way, but believers in Rome were doing just that.

If a member of one of these Roman churches could somehow be transported to a plateaued or declining congregation in America today, the envy and rivalry there would likely be familiar. The churches were divided then the same way they are today. Some of them preached Christ sincerely, eager to see people come into the kingdom of God. Others preached insincerely, using the gospel to further their own selfish purposes. These false teachers might have belonged to some kind of legalistic wing of the church that opposed Paul's ministry to the Gentiles and his emphasis on the grace of God instead of obedience to Jewish law.

Humility is one of the great secret weapons of spiritual power. Envy and strife go together just as love and unity go together. Self-righteousness and pride are two of the greatest threats to spiritual health and church growth. "Do nothing out of rivalry or conceit," Paul advises, "but in humility consider others as more important than yourselves" (2:3). Paul's critics were out to promote themselves and win a following of their own. I'm sure you won't have any trouble thinking of certain televangelists who build their own personal empires including private jets and luxury homes and then implore viewers to keep supporting them. More to the point is that churches get caught up in doing work for their own selfish reasons, not for the purpose of building God's kingdom.

Paul's aim was to glorify Christ and get others to follow Him too, while his critics were out to divide the church for their own benefit. Instead of asking, "Have you trusted Christ?" they demanded, "Whose side are you on, ours or Paul's?" Today's struggling churches know that tactic well. The people who practice it need to realize they are only hurting themselves.

Churches on the road to rebuilding have to stop and take an honest look at their motives: "Why do we do what we do? What's the bottom-line motive for our programming, our staffing, and our ministries?"

One of the key issues that bubbles to the surface here is ownership. Unfortunately many people feel that the church belongs to them. They often talk about "our church" or "my church." The problem with this is that ownership often leads to control, and control typically leads to manipulation. The church simply does not belong to any individual or subgroup no matter how powerful, persuasive, or pushy they are.

Who owns the church? God does! But while we're quick to shout out the correct answer, our actions and attitudes may show that the answer in our hearts is something quite different. What motives underlie those actions? Are we here to serve the Lord and promote His agenda, or are we here for something else?

In his book *Mere Christianity*, the great British lay theologian C. S. Lewis calls pride "the great sin . . . the essential vice, the utmost evil. . . . Unchastity, anger, greed, drunkenness, and all that, are mere fleabites in comparison: it was through Pride that the devil became the devil: Pride leads to every other vice: it is the complete anti-God state of mind." Strong, powerful, harsh words. And yet, if you think about it, pride is at the root of pretty much everything a man or a church does that is wrongheaded. Glance at the headlines in today's newspaper, and chances are that every crime took place because somebody was convinced he deserved something that he didn't have. Pride derails our motives. It makes us think, *This is all about me, my opinions and others who share them, my goals and desires, my money, my plans for the future.* No, it's not.

We're called to be humble the way Christ was humble. The Son of Man left the form of God and His home in heaven to take the form of a man on Earth, subject to the same discomforts and inconveniences as the rest of the world. As Paul expressed it so powerfully, Jesus "emptied Himself by assuming the form of a slave, taking on the likeness of men. . . . He humbled Himself by becoming obedient to the point of death—even to death on a cross" (2:7–8). Crucifixion was such a gruesome torture that it was against the law for Roman citizens to be executed that way. Christ left the perfect peace and comfort of heaven to die an agonizing death on the cross for sinners even though He was without sin. That's humility. That's our model.

Respect and Relevance

Another point Paul makes in his letter to the Philippians is that churches must be dedicated to bringing glory to the Lord by the *way* they worship. In the end Paul observed, "What does it matter? Just that in every way, whether out of false motives or true, Christ is proclaimed" (1:18). In other words, even false motives can result in spiritual truth as long as Christ is the center of the worship experience. The gospel message can survive intact even when the messengers aren't entirely true to the faith.

It should be our earnest prayer that nothing we do, say, or think brings reproach on the cause of Christ. Those of us in the ministry ought to hope for this beyond anything else. Every day we must seek the guidance of God's Holy Spirit so that we will in no way be ashamed of what we do or bring shame to Him. I believe this means we need to examine our method of worship. Some say that the method doesn't matter as long as the message is right. I disagree. I believe that some methods are unworthy of the gospel. They are cheap whereas the gospel is a costly message that required the death of God's only Son. Is the way we worship pleasing to the Lord? Does it bring shame upon Him in any form or fashion? If our churches are going to be relevant in this twenty-first century, we must have biblically based direction with a methodology that is totally biblical as well.

One aspect of methodology that has set off countless worship wars and weakened or torpedoed countless churches is the turmoil over service music. There are huge emotional battles on the topics of musical selection and worship style. Too many churches to list have split over the music issue. Some church leaders today believe this is the greatest crisis facing American Protestants today. After discussing the issue on his *Focus on the Family* radio show, Dr. James Dobson observed, "Of all the subjects we've ever covered in this radio program, from abortion to pornography to whatever, the most controversial subject we've ever dealt with is music. You can make people mad about music more quickly than anything else." Though the intensity of the argument seems to have increased in recent years, this battle has gone on for generations now in some places. According to pastor Rick Warren, Charles Spurgeon called his music ministry "the War Department."

The church at Philippi probably didn't sing at all or have any sort of music during their services, though music was a popular way to praise God at other times. The Psalms were, of course, written to be sung, and the Scripture frequently mentions musical praise. While we have no idea what the music sounded like (there was no musical notation then), the Bible regularly mentions drums, cymbals, trumpets, tambourines, harps, and other instruments beginning in early Old Testament times. Traditional hymn singing to an instrumental accompaniment during a church service has been around for hundreds of years, though at first it was condemned for its worldliness. Even such beloved pieces as "Silent Night" and the "Hallelujah" chorus from *The Messiah* were criticized as radical and inappropriate for worship when they were introduced.

Healthy, growing churches in every region of the country have traditional music every week. Equally strong and successful churches across the nation use contemporary music. The worship experience in these two kinds of churches may be different, but the objective and the result are the same: proclaiming the gospel of Christ and worshipping Him joyfully.

Nevertheless, choosing or changing the style of music is often the most volatile experience in the life of a congregation. Music helps each of us as individuals define who we are. There's a vast range of strongly held beliefs and opinions, often shaped over a lifetime, that determine what we like and what we think is appropriate for worship. If people look first at what honors God and lifts up His gospel message, they'll come to an agreement, and the issue of what kind of music to use will be settled with a minimum of wailing and gnashing of teeth. If people look first at what they like and what they think the church should do, it's a good sign that the fireworks are not far behind.

Churches have a long tradition of supporting the musical arts, and until the 1960s one American church played more or less the same music as another. The main components of church music then were an organ, a choir dressed in matching robes, and congregational hymns from the hymnbook. Then came the folk music era and the Woodstock generation that didn't connect with organs and more formal musical styles of the past. So churches began introducing contemporary music and instrumentation into their services: guitars, drum sets, and keyboards replaced the organs while lyrics projected on a screen replaced hymnbooks in the pews.

Some churchgoers were outraged and others were delighted. The battle has raged ever since. Taylors First Baptist Church, where I serve as pastor, unapologetically utilizes both traditional and contemporary music. When you think about it, "Christian music" really doesn't describe a musical style but rather a musical message. It rightly includes everything from Gregorian chant and Renaissance motets to hard rock with Christian lyrics from groups like POD and Relient K (ask your kids).

In *The Purpose Driven Church,* Rick Warren explains that his church decided on the contemporary approach and has never looked back. A survey showed that people who came to his services at Saddleback Community Church overwhelmingly listened to middle-of-the-road adult contemporary music. After learning that, Rick writes, "We made the strategic decision to stop singing hymns in our seeker services. Within a year of deciding what would be 'our sound,' Saddleback *exploded* with growth. I will admit that we have lost hundreds of potential members because of the style of music Saddleback uses. On the other hand, we have attracted thousands more because of our music."[4]

The prospect of change in music and worship style is a potential flash point. However, the essential question is this: Does the music under consideration (or under fire) honor the Lord? Have you convinced yourself that your own personal style preference is blessed of God? And does that mean that other styles are not blessed by God? This kind of musical snobbery has destroyed a lot of churches and hindered others. My contention is that many types of music can be used by the Lord if their content is biblical, the performers are spiritual, and the inner motivation is truly one of seeking worship.

The same holds true for church architecture; the way you dress on Sunday morning; whether you pray kneeling, sitting, or jumping up and down; and almost every other aspect of the worship experience. Does your church honor God and seek to know, serve, and obey Him? If you do, everything else will fall into place. But the church has to move past its self-centeredness and cultivate a Christlike humility.

The Peace of God

If only Christians would pay close attention to Paul's warning against self-righteousness, so many problems would evaporate on the spot! As the *Holman Bible Handbook* points out in its commentary on Paul, Christians are called to work out their salvation with fear and trembling, not with complaining and friction. The advice Paul gives is practical, but it's based on unshakable faith and clear focus on Jesus: "Paul's joy was grounded in Christ, as is all of life."[5]

Near the end of his letter to the church at Philippi, Paul wrote, "Finally brothers, whatever is true, whatever is honorable, whatever is just, whatever is pure, whatever is lovely, whatever is commendable—if there is any moral excellence and if there is any praise—dwell on these things. Do what you have learned and received and heard and seen in me, and the God of peace will be with you" (4:8–9).

In shrinking churches, the peace of God is typically in short supply, the focus is fuzzy, and the problems seem too plentiful and too tenacious to get hold of. Grab onto Jesus as the core and foundation of your church. Then look around at the specific challenges that are stunting your growth. Some of them you can change, and some you can't. Your next step, then, is to fix the things you can and figure out how, with God's help, to grow over, under, and through the things you can't.

Facing the Facts

As far as we know, the church in Philippi was not in a panic when Paul wrote to them. They weren't crying out for assistance in the midst of some sort of emergency. In fact, they didn't ask for help at all; Paul, imprisoned probably in Rome and thinking of their well-being, took the initiative on his own.

So evidently the Philippian church didn't have any major problems. Good for them. If only it were the same in churches today. Every congregation has a list of challenges, surprises, difficulties, and irritants that it has to deal with. Any of these can stunt a church's growth. While the list will be different for each congregation, two factors will be the same.

First, the solution to every problem begins by laying personal preferences aside and putting Christ first. Once you recognize that Jesus is the center of your worship experience, many crises will disappear on the spot, and others will fade into the background. We've already looked at Paul's admonition to the Philippians about honoring God first and what C. S. Lewis and others have said about the sheer destructive force of pride: it will shrivel your church faster than salt on a slug. You must face it and overcome it.

In other words, keep your opinions to yourself. Are you anticipating a knockdown drag-out over music like so many congregations have had in recent years? Ask this question: What music honors God? Unsure of your commitment to mission work? What gives the most glory to the Lord? Replace self-serving pride with humility as Christ was humble, and you'll go a long way toward minimizing or settling the issues. If the problem doesn't disappear, lifting up Christ above all is still the shortest pathway to the right solution.

Second, as I mentioned earlier, realize that every church faces two kinds of problems: the kind you can fix and the kind you can't. For the fixable ones, bring your humility to the meeting room and get together on a plan of action to change the situation. For the ones you can't change, look for God's guidance in plotting a way to circumvent them, blow them up, or mow them down.

Uncontrollables

When I came to the church I now serve as pastor, I quickly discovered that several of the factors contributing to our church's long, slow decline were situations we couldn't do anything about. These are variables the research teams call "uncontrollable." Two of our biggest uncontrollables were challenges a lot of shrinking churches will know well.

First, we were an old church. Taylors First Baptist was founded in 1864 and has a rich and wonderful history behind it. But because of that, it's also statistically likely to be a plateauing or declining church and when I got there, it was fulfilling that mission admirably. It was a true example of the studies indicating that the younger a congregation is, the more likely it is to grow. Once it's older and the founders pass responsibility on to the next generation of leaders, a church tends to start losing momentum. We were a textbook case of a glorious past being one of the greatest impediments to growth in the present and future. There seems to be a window of about twenty years or so early in the life of a church when everybody is energized and excited and anything seems possible. After that the focus and vision are more likely to start getting fuzzy. Little fiefdoms develop, and members develop a loyalty to certain people and traditions that overshadows their loyalty to the Bible.

People tend to forget why they do things, going through the motions out of habit or tradition. A fresh look at the situation might reveal this is something that should be done differently or not done at all. Years ago some behavioral specialists put four monkeys in a laboratory enclosure with a step stool in it. Whenever one of the monkeys climbed on top of the stool, all the monkeys got a mild electric shock. Soon they learned not to climb on the stool. Then the specialists replaced one of the monkeys with a new one who didn't know about the shock. When he started for the stool, the other monkeys pulled him away so they wouldn't be jolted. One at a time over several days, all the monkeys were replaced. Even after all the original monkeys were gone and none of the new ones had ever been shocked, they still stayed off the stool and kept newcomers from climbing it. They didn't know why they should stay off the stool; they only knew they weren't supposed to go there.

In describing tradition-driven churches, Rick Warren notes that their rallying cry is, "We've always done it this way." He goes on to say, "The goal of a tradition-driven church is to simply perpetuate the past. Change is almost always seen as negative, and stagnation is interpreted as 'stability.' Older churches tend to be bound together by rules, regulations, and rituals. . . . In some churches, tradition can be such a driving force that everything else, even God's will, becomes secondary."[6]

Gene Mims identifies The Legacy Church as one of *The Seven Churches Not in the Book of Revelation*. These churches "are generally adorned with plaques, pictures, and pretty stained glass windows (memorialized, of course)." They remind Gene of petrified wood: "They used to be wood, and now they're gradually getting to be like rock."[7] These churches have a tendency to focus constantly on the great and glorious days of the past, always trying to preserve the memories and somehow recapturing the feel of those historic moments.

Certainly the past has its place. It's appropriate to honor those who have gone before, and history can often teach us how to do things better in the future. The problem comes when a constant focus on glories of the past blinds a church to the needs and opportunities of the present. Rather than becoming a springboard to growth, history becomes an anchor that drags a congregation down. If someone isn't connected somehow with the storied past, they'll probably never find a place in the church where they fit in and feel comfortable. There's no hunger within the church leadership to reach more people on the road ahead with the gospel because all the attention is focused in the rearview mirror.

Embrace the past, celebrate it, thank God for it, and for God's sake move on!

The other important variable we couldn't do anything about when I came to Taylors was the location of our church. I realize there are cases when churches have literally sold their property in one neighborhood and moved somewhere else. For most congregations that's not possible or even necessary, but once in a while it makes sense. The most common instance of a complete relocation is probably when an old neighborhood becomes entirely commercial or industrial over the years and no one lives nearby any more. Members will stay loyal for a while once they move, but gradually they'll find churches closer to their new homes and start going there instead. Younger folks with no emotional attachment to the church will transfer their memberships even quicker. There are instances where a church has been physically isolated by urban renewal or separated from the surrounding area by a freeway. In one case a small but active church near Nashville was separated from its members after a new lake was formed in front of it by the Army Corps of Engineers! Under these drastic conditions, the only choice may be to pull up stakes and go where the people are.

Usually the situation isn't that extreme, but location has a big effect on growth potential. No-growth churches are less often in the leafy suburbs and more often where there is a transitional neighborhood, poverty, or a great influx of other religions traditions. Our church in Taylors found itself in an old mill village that had long ago ceased to be a vibrant part of the community. The neighborhood once thrived as the textile industry grew during the Industrial Revolution when thousands of people came from the surrounding area to work in row upon row of spinning and weaving mills. In the last twenty or thirty years, that industry has relocated largely overseas, the factories have closed, and the workers have moved away. While our church is within reach of growing areas, it is hard to find and located between railroad tracks that make expansion difficult and the noise level high.

We can't help being where we are, but we can help how we feel about it. A good attitude in the face of all the facts is an indispensable tool for building a growing church. If you can't come up with a positive attitude anywhere else, remember what Paul wrote in Philippians 1:6: "I am sure of this, that He who started a good work in you will carry it on to completion until the day of Christ Jesus." God was behind the founding of your church no matter where it is, and He will not abandon you now. He may not show Himself on your terms where and when and how you want it, but He's there working with your church according to His perfect plan. Not your plan and not the deacons' plan—His plan.

Clearing the Pathway

Then there are the factors you *can* change. Let's look at those for a moment. The potential is to heave those rocks out of the pathway to growth. The challenge is to do it without setting off a landslide of hurt feelings, turf wars, and other problems.

No one understood the hazards of church growth better than Donald McGavran, who's widely considered to be the first person ever to study the topic in detail. A third-generation missionary, he was born in India in 1897 and spent much of his career overseas. His 1959 book *How Churches Grow* marked the beginning of the modern church growth movement. McGavran was amazed to discover that growth, which he considered good and healthy and essential, generated tension within congregations. In a letter to his wife in 1961, he wrote, "It is clear that emphasizing the growth of the church divides the camp. It is really a divisive topic. How strange when we are all presumably disciples of the Lord Jesus Christ." I'd say nothing much has changed since then.

One major growth-inhibiting factor that churches can change but which often "divides the camp" is power structures that have developed within the church and are out to preserve the status quo at all costs. Often this becomes a family or small group that has taken control of a church's decision-making process over the years. When new people come into the church, or a new pastor starts bringing in fresh faces, these "strangers," unaligned with any camp, threaten the existing power centers.

In this case the ruling elite often take steps—above board in the light of day, underhanded and sneaky, or a combination of the two—either to remove/sabotage the pastor or make sure that he and the new people he attracts are excluded from decision making and participation in leadership. Sometimes it's a particular group of friends with deep roots in the church that has run the show for decades. Sometimes it's a single distinguished family, an extended family, or a tight little cluster of families (often generous donors) who are convinced that their long association with the church and their material generosity entitle them to call the shots. After all, nobody knows better than they do what's best for the church. A wise pastor will always seek to identify clearly the power structure within the body of believers. He also needs to be careful to discern between the formal structure and the actual power sources. There is often a major difference!

The problem of an entrenched ruling elite comes up time and again in growth studies. A 1991 report by the Southern Baptist Convention noted, "Change is an unnatural act in many churches.

Every church has its 'root guards' and 'turf protectors' who are out in force any time a basic assumption is questioned or threatened." Another church growth commentator, Hollis L. Green, wrote that for many struggling congregations "church has become imprisoned by the pattern of previous generations."

Gene Mims calls this kind of church the Family Chapel:

> The people who attend these churches are either related or act like they are. In fact, when it comes to Family Chapels you can never really join. You can be born into one or you can marry into one, but you cannot truly join one. You can attend one and belong as a member, but you can't feel a part of the church unless there is a way you can enter through a relationship. The members of Family Chapels have feelings for one another that cannot be described to an outsider. . . .
>
> Family Chapels are usually dominated by a family or two with a ruling patriarch or matriarch who pretty much runs the show. The Family Chapel has trouble assimilating new members and in fact will band together in any crisis, especially those that come against any of the "family." One pastor put it this way. "We grew the numbers with new people, we changed the worship service, we built a new building—and they got a new [pastor]. We had no business meetings, we had no deacon meetings. Didn't have to. Because the 'patriarch committee' made all the decisions."[8]

These kinds of "patriarch led" churches come in all shapes and sizes. Some of them are big, prominent churches in major metropolitan areas. And some of them grow in spite of themselves. Their goal should be to take the primary focus off the leading families and venerable history of the church and put Jesus Christ in first place again. It won't be easy or without sacrifice, but in the long haul it's the way to a church that is healthy to the core.

Good-bye to Sacred Cows

Another growth impediment churches can fix is program paralysis. When a church fails to maintain relevant programs, it develops a lethargy that destroys growth. We've already seen how a lot of American churches seem to be lost in the 1950s. Their mantra is, "Try nothing new! Change nothing! Keep doing it the good old-fashioned way!"

It's almost impossible to imagine a schoolteacher today running her classroom using nothing but a blackboard and fifty-year-old books, and making disruptive children sit in the corner wearing a dunce cap unless she decided to swat them on the backside with her ruler instead. That's not the way we conduct school any more. There are better ways to get the job done, and students and parents have different expectations from their counterparts of the 1950s. Yet some churches don't bat an eye at using tired, obsolete, irrelevant programs to spread the good news to their twenty-first-century neighborhoods.

When these creaky old programs started, they were no doubt the latest thing. Now they're transformed into sacred cows, out-of-date but woven deeply into the fabric of the congregation. New-member prospects don't have the shared history to appreciate them, so they don't see the point. It may be that some outreach or Sunday school was started by a revered member of a past generation, or it's named after the founder's granddaughter. These are all honorable ways to mark accomplishments of the past, but the church can't allow them to overshadow its mission. They can solve this problem by taking a hard, honest look at what they're doing and whether or not it makes sense to someone on the outside.

That's not to say this is an easy fix. Some of the current members may mount a heroic counterattack against any effort to modify or discontinue "their" program. This is a good subject for some heartfelt prayer. It might be wise to transition slowly out of a program over a year or two. But with God's help you'll get through it. Probably.

Breaking the Holy Huddle

While the Bible consistently teaches that the Word of God is absolute and never changing, it also tells us that we as Christians have to be flexible in our approach based on whom we're approaching. Stagnant churches resist being flexible because they've developed outreach prejudice. This is the tendency to reach out only to people like themselves who are obviously like-minded or compatible. This factor destroys growth, particularly when a neighborhood begins to change from one ethnic, economic, or social group to another. The church becomes a holy huddle of persons who think alike, look alike, and bemoan the fact that their type of people no longer live near the church house.

The fields are white with harvest, but these churchgoers don't care for the crop. There's corn and cucumbers everywhere, and all they want is tomatoes. Reaching out to this changing audience might mean coming to grips with a stereotype of the new residents or even re-thinking something as fundamental as the time of the service to make them feel welcome. Without ignoring its roots, a church has to branch out in new directions and cultivate new tastes.

Time and again Paul teaches his followers that they should preach to Jews as well as Gentiles and to people of every sort of background, not just the ones who agree with them or hang on to the old way of doing things.

> For although I am free from all people, I have made myself a slave to all, in order to win more people. To the Jews I became like a Jew, to win Jews; to those under the law, like one under the law—though I myself am not under the law—to win those under the law. To those who are outside the law,

> like one outside the law—not being outside God's law, but under the law of Christ—to win those outside the law. To the weak I became weak, in order to win the weak. I have become all things to all people, so that I may by all means save some. Now I do all this because of the gospel, that I may become a partner in its benefits. (1 Cor. 9:19–23)

Cultural differences are secondary to Christian spiritual unity. As one commentator pointed out, "Biblical church growth emphasizes Christ, not culture." Yes, it's important to meet new prospective members at their point of need and explain the gospel in terms they're comfortable with. It's also important to remember that those differences never have to stand in the way of our shared commitment to Jesus.

Dr. Thom Rainer, president of LifeWay Christian Resources, has done an admirable job of pointing out many characteristics of churches that have been able to pull out of a decline. Few others tread this path; most would rather deal with church plants and what has made them grow or with churches that have virtually died and been resurrected from the dead. Few sources deal with how to transition a church without absolutely removing its core, destroying its history, and starting from scratch. Chapter 4 of his book *Simple Church,* written with Eric Geiger, outlines the stories of three churches that have bucked the trend against shrinking by focusing on Christ above all and developing clear and simple objectives that reflect His calling.

Three Simple Stories

Immanuel Baptist Church in Glasgow, Kentucky, doubled in size from 150 to 300 members in two years, even though the population of the city remained about the same, after the church leaders realized they had to continue teaching and maturing new people once they got involved. They identified a need to move visitors to membership and then into in-depth Bible study through small groups. This gave the newcomers a deeper appreciation for the ministry and mission of the church and encouraged them to settle in and find a place of service. In other words, these leaders saw how important it was to draw people from the outer circle to the inner circle and give them a sense of belonging.

Christ Fellowship in Miami, a longtime fixture in the neighborhood where members were generally happy with the status quo, reorganized their weekly program to promote a "growing and intimate relationship with God." They set up ministry teams and encouraged members to invite their relatives and neighbors to church in their community, where seventy nationalities were represented. Old programs that didn't fit the new direction, including Sunday night worship, were discontinued in order to devote time, space, and funding to programs that served the community more effectively. Somehow they managed to get rid of their sacred cows without having a brawl over them. The results were a newly energized spirit in the eighty-nine-year-old church, hundreds of new members immersed in small-group Bible study, and a strong increase in youth participation.

Unlike these two examples, Northpoint Community Church in Alpharetta, Georgia, didn't have a slow-growth history to overcome. In fact, it had no history at all. The founding pastor, Andy Stanley, and his leadership team decided from the beginning to have a simple organization aimed at bringing people "into the kitchen," in other words, into the spiritual heart of the congregation. In ten years Northpoint grew from a handful of founding members to more than sixteen thousand.[9]

Change transforms churches, but for various reasons some churches steadfastly resist looking at their policies and programs in a new light. Leaders who try to guide a church under those conditions have a treacherous path ahead of them. Shrinking churches that don't want to change tend to chew up pastors at a high rate.

Faced with opposition to growth, responsible and visionary leaders either give in, give up, or get out. A pastor's participation is one of the most important components in getting a church to grow. How the pastor sees his role and how he responds to the pressure have a major effect on both his career and the future prospects for his troubled congregation.

Shrink-proof Leadership

The incredible shrinking church needs visionary, tireless, articulate, inspiring leadership to steer it off the old pathway and onto a new and more promising one. A struggling congregation has to have a pastor willing to lead the charge, to do things differently in the future than in the past. Virtually every church-growth survey tells us that the role of the pastor cannot be overestimated. His heart, passion, skill set, and personal agenda will have more impact on a church's attitude and growth potential than any other single factor. He has to take a lead role in bringing the church back to good health.

Because of his high profile, the pastor is an easy target. Once a church decides to set off in a new direction, the first order of business is often to sack the pastor and bring in somebody else. Years ago I heard someone discussing renewal in the church say that a pastor may not be the key to positive change, but he can be the lock. Ouch. A declining church is probably going to have a preacher that people see as the captain who sank the ship. This causes many frustrated worshippers to believe that before their church will ever grow again they'll have to have a new pastor. Many pastors believe the same thing. Once the winds of change begin to blow around the worship center, they start cranking out resumes.

Calling a new pastor is a natural reaction for a church getting ready to change course. Some pastors do stay too long. Sometimes it takes a change of leadership to break old mind-sets and replace them with fresh ones. A pastor may see change as a threat to his power or influence and therefore selfishly fight to keep things the same. In other cases, church leaders have long-established habits, preconceptions, or prejudices that cloud their judgment in the present and their vision for the future. And we all know cases where dedicated Christian warriors who have spent decades leading a church resist admitting that the time has come for them to hand over the reins to the next generation.

Sometimes, however, getting a new pastor to lead a church transition is not the best move in the long run. Writers Jere Allen and Kirk Hadaway report research that shows 22 percent of breakout churches—churches that experienced a big attendance spurt after years of little or no growth—had the same pastor both during the plateau period and the times of significant increase. Pastors have been able to break out of their own malaise and inspire the congregation to do the same.

Successful Pastors Stay Planted

In his book *Breakout Churches,* Thom Rainer goes into great detail to support his point that changing pastors is not a step churches necessarily have to take on the road to growth. On the contrary, he suggests churches that call a new pastor every few years are more likely to be struggling than churches where pastors invest a long season of their careers. Thom has spent nearly twenty years studying how and why churches grow, including serving as dean of the Billy Graham School of Missions, Evangelism, and Church Growth at Southern Baptist Theological Seminary. This book offers both general and specific research that indicates holding on to your pastor through a time of great change is usually a good idea.

> We have noted for years in our research that a direct correlation is present between pastoral tenure and evangelical effectiveness in churches. But this contrast is striking. The average tenure of a breakout church leader exceeds twenty-one years, while the other pastors in our study have been at their churches only about four years. . . .
>
> On the one hand, pastors are often quick to leave a church when a seemingly better, sometimes bigger, opportunity comes their way. While we cannot and will not question God's call on any one pastor when it comes to moves, we cannot help but be concerned about the overall trend in quick moves. A pastor of one of our comparison churches said: "I have made five moves to what I thought were greener pastures. If I had stayed at my first or even second church, I believe that church would be very healthy today, and I would be more content. I just wish somehow I could communicate this message to younger pastors."
>
> On the other hand, churches and their lay leaders can be incredibly demanding of, if not vicious to, pastors. In my consulting ministry with the Rainer Group, I often deal with lay leaders who treat pastors like CEOs and expect immediate results of them. And ironically, while these lay leaders demand quick results, they can be reluctant to give the pastor any authority to carry out the initiatives they expect to take place. The result is frustration for both parties. No wonder it is not uncommon to see pastors leave under pressure or even be forcefully terminated in such situations.
>
> Long pastoral tenure is not a panacea or the single answer to struggling churches across America, but I believe that long tenure is *one* of the key requisites for churches to move from mediocrity to goodness to greatness.[10]

As a specific example, Rainer looks at The Temple Church in Nashville, which formed in 1977. The church founded a Christian school and started an outreach to the community. By the early 1980s the congregation had built a multimillion-dollar facility and saw attendance climb to one thousand per week. Then the church plateaued and started a slow decline: an attendance average of 904 the next year, then 900, then 876. By 1990 the number was 659.

That was when the founding pastor, Michael Lee Graves, had what he called a "vision" of reaching out to all races, ethnic groups, and nationalities in his melting-pot neighborhood and not concentrating on his existing membership of middle- and upper-income blacks. The church was out of room and needed a larger meeting space, but Graves believed the trouble was more than a matter of a new building. When Graves shared his vision with a core of three hundred church members, they threatened to withhold their financial support if he carried out his plans. Trusting God to lead him, Graves stuck to his guns. The three hundred left the church, setting off a short-term financial crisis that forced Temple to close its school and sending Graves to the hospital with exhaustion.

The members that were left focused on the new vision God had given them. In two years average weekly attendance was back over one thousand. Ten years after that, attendance reached three thousand a week. Same leader, same neighborhood, but a new focus, vision, and passion for reaching the community for Christ.

Members as Friends

In order to resuscitate a declining church, pastors and other leaders have to commit themselves wholeheartedly to the task. Maintaining a surface relationship with the members and going through the motions isn't enough to do the job. If others don't see you putting everything you have into building a better church, why should they? Growth-minded pastors cultivate deep, sincere relationships with as many church members as possible, which establishes foundations for tackling the challenges of change together. If pastors can communicate effectively with the church and make sure the lines of communication stay open in both directions, and if they can earn and hold the members' trust, then they can step out in a new direction knowing that plenty of people will follow them. Otherwise they're liable to look around after a while and discover that everybody else decided the unfamiliar path was too risky.

In other words, when a pastor wants to lead the church in a new direction, the chance of success is far greater when the members are also his friends. People respond better to a friend: "That's not some self-absorbed pastor up there telling me what to do and pushing his own agenda; that's my friend."

Even so, relationship building is no guarantee that a pastor's revolutionary idea will capture the hearts and minds of his congregation. Michael Lee Graves learned that the hard way when he set out to expand his church's reach. Hundreds of supporters suddenly became former supporters. But he always communicated well, and he always followed through on what he said he would do.

One thing I encourage pastors to do, whatever the size of their churches, is to be personally involved as much as possible in the lives of their people. In this age of impersonal electronic communication, a genuine personal letter is like a little present delivered by the mailman. I write personal letters every week to members of my church. I write to every member who has lost a spouse the week before the first anniversary of that loss. I also write personal notes before Mother's Day and Father's Day to every member who has lost that parent in the past year. Until our membership climbed above one thousand, I used to call members on their birthdays.

Making the extra effort to extend a personal word of greeting, congratulation, or condolence brings results way beyond what the effort requires. So few people get this kind of attention any more, especially from people they perceive as leaders, that a personal note from the preacher is a real treat. For them to get mail means they are important enough that the pastor carves out time to write them. Yes, it's one more task a busy pastor has to squeeze into a day that's already packed full. But after a little practice, it's amazing how many cards you can do in thirty or forty-five uninterrupted minutes.

Jimmy Draper is by acclamation one of the most successful leaders in the history of the Southern Baptist Convention. His churches grew and prospered. He preceded me some years past as president of the Convention and built the Baptist Sunday School Board, now known as LifeWay Christian Resources, into a thriving $400-million-per-year-plus ministry tool with a respected presence around the world. From the time he first started moving in the wider denominational and evangelical world in the late 1950s, Jimmy was one of the U. S. Postal Service's best customers. He wrote letters to everybody all the time. Busy as he was pastoring a church and, ultimately, leading fifteen million Southern Baptists, he made time to dash off a line or two whenever he thought it would help or encourage somebody.

As computers made their way into his life, he didn't quit writing letters, but he did reach even more people personally by adding e-mail to his communication repertoire. He kept up a steady stream of paper mail just like always, but on top of that, people who e-mailed him got an e-mail back, almost always on the same day. Certainly Jimmy has many wonderful and God-given leadership skills; it's not that writing letters made him successful. But I don't think he would have had the same reputation or the same track record without that commitment to personal relationships.

One final note on the story: There must have been six or seven hundred guests at Jimmy's retirement celebration not long ago. At one point the master of ceremonies asked everyone in the room who had ever received a personal letter from Jimmy to raise their hand. Probably 90 percent of the people put a hand in the air. The memento all the guests took home that night was an inscribed letter opener. It was the perfect souvenir to honor his ministry.

Listen to Leaders

Pastors have to take special care to communicate and cultivate relationships with their leaders. I believe it's extremely important that your governing body—deacons, elders, vestry, session, etc.—see you as their friend. I make this a strong part of my ministry and even state it as an expectation for all new deacons. Friends can disagree, but friends always love each other. The greater goal of building relationships is an attitude of trust on the part of the congregation. Many pastors begin to push for substantial changes in programming, budgeting, and other areas long before they have built a trust relationship. You can't do that. You have to earn the right to lead people in a new direction or start changing aspects of the church that others put in place.

This calls for restraint, and it can be tough to bide your time and hold your tongue just when you most need to do it. The vision strikes, or you land at a new church. You see the problems and pitfalls, and naturally you want to hit the ground running and start taking care of them. But wait. Who are you? What gives you the right to make these changes? Give folks a little time, let them get to know and trust you, and then implementing the vision will be far easier and more likely to succeed.

That being said, a new pastor may need to change some things on a fast track, and he can hope to do those early on while the honeymoon period is still in effect. These kinds of changes involve clear emergencies that the church has to deal with immediately in order to stop the free fall or prevent a major new step in the wrong direction.

Wise pastors set two goals for themselves in the first year of a new pastorate: to learn and to love. They're simple aims but so important. Pastors tend to be talkers, which is essential for them in their work. But when it comes to establishing yourself and becoming part of a new community of faith, you can't learn much with your mouth open. A pastor must listen to and feel the history and tradition of the church, sit down for leisurely conversations with members, look through records, and chat with other people in the community. As they spend time learning what is truly going on within the church body, new pastors start developing loving, caring relationships, making clear to the church body that every one of them is important. Learn and love. These are the means necessary for rebuilding a church no matter what the specific steps are.

Casting the Vision

Along with building individual relationships inside the church, pastors have to establish an overall public image or persona as the leader of the church. How a pastor presents himself publicly is extremely important. Obviously this image should be an outgrowth of his private personality, but there are several characteristics to emphasize. Virtually every expert will tell you that the pastor must be a constant "caster of the vision." In other words, the congregation and the world must see him as a person who is passionate about what he believes God has led the church to do.

Rick Warren emphasizes this in *The Purpose Driven Church*. In fact he says, and I agree, that the pastor ought to lift up that vision once a month. He recalls the story in the book of Nehemiah that tells of people rebuilding the wall around Jerusalem. When they were halfway through, their enemies the Ammonites found out what they were doing and plotted to stop them from finishing the work. Nehemiah stepped boldly in, reminding his followers what they were doing and why, and promising to protect and guide them:

> I stationed people behind the lower sections of the wall, at the vulnerable areas. I stationed them by families with their swords, spears, and bows. After I made an inspection, I stood up and said to the nobles, the officials, and the rest of the people, "Don't be afraid of them. Remember the great and

> awe-inspiring Lord, and fight for your countrymen, your sons and daughters, your wives and homes. . . . Our God will fight for us." (Neh. 4:13–14, 20)

Rick points out that twenty-six days into the building project the people felt threatened and needed reassurance. That's when Nehemiah renewed the vision. The story leads to what Rick calls the Nehemiah Principle: "Vision and purpose must be restated every twenty-six days to keep the church moving in the right direction." This supports the idea that pastors should communicate the purpose and focus of the church at least once a month. He adds, "It is amazing how quickly human beings—and churches—lose their sense of purpose."[11] You've probably sensed that yourself if you stop to think about it. Church activities compete with all the other responsibilities and distractions of modern culture. It's easy to take them as they come and not think too much about the vision behind them. With no understanding of a vision, pretty soon you forget why all that church stuff is there to begin with. And as Solomon warned us, without vision the people perish.

What does this "recasting the vision" mean in practical terms? Remind your governing or advisory body at least once a month of your vision for the church and of specific plans you have for preserving, enhancing, and extending that vision. Make it one of the first things you tell the leadership when you come to the pastorate, and come back to it time and again to keep it fresh and in the forefront of everything you do as a church. Having a vision for the church makes every other decision easier. Does whatever opportunity or change you're considering enhance or advance the vision of the church? If so, you should probably do it. If not, you should probably let it go.

Founded on Christ

Let me clarify one important point. We're talking about church growth, but if your objective is just to get the attendance numbers up, you will probably not succeed in building your church. If you do, it will be a temporary improvement at best. To grow securely, a church first has to be spiritually vital and strong. Relationships, vision, and all the rest are the means to help your church grow numerically, but they do it ultimately by strengthening and deepening the faith of a body of believers. If all you want is a full house, arrange a screening of a currently popular Hollywood movie or give away a motorcycle. I emphasize repeatedly to my leaders and staff that a spiritually healthy church is the final goal. A healthy church will grow, and that growth will be solid and long lasting.

As much as some pastors hesitate to admit it, a church doesn't have to have lots of property or financial resources to be healthy. It doesn't have to be filled with prominent community leaders or old established families (though there's nothing wrong with any of this). A healthy church comes from a foundation built on the worship of Jesus Christ, as Paul wrote in his first letter to the church at Corinth:

> Brothers, consider your calling; not many are wise from a human perspective, not many powerful, not many of noble birth. Instead, God has chosen the world's foolish things to shame the wise, and God has chosen the world's weak things to shame the strong. God has chosen the world's insignificant and despised things—the things viewed as nothing—so He might bring to nothing the things that are viewed as something, so that no one can boast in His presence. But from Him you are in Christ Jesus, who for us became wisdom from God, as well as righteousness, sanctification, and redemption, in order that, as it is written: The one who boasts must boast in the Lord. (1 Cor. 1:26–31)

Donald McGavran had a simpler way to express the same thought: "Remember that at the heart of the Church Growth Movement here or anywhere in the world is the Great Commission," which is Jesus' marching orders to His disciples in the book of

Matthew to "make disciples of all nations . . ." (28:19). The message here is that a church's primary goal is to spread the gospel to the ends of the earth; if we stay true to that, Jesus will be with us from now on. Will Jesus break His promise? Will He allow churches that obey Him to decline? I don't think so.

Leading in Love

It's a pastor's responsibility to maintain the focus and keep the lines of communication open. I believe it's just as important to intersperse all those exhortations and directives with a rhythm of strong, positive affirmation. I try to present a balance. A pastor has to lead with authority, but at the same time he needs to be strongly affirming with the congregation. Ephesians 4:15 tells us as Christians to speak the truth in love. There must be times when the pastor strongly exhorts the congregation because of their lack of faithfulness, commitment, or evangelistic fervor. But these words have to have the right context, the right perspective.

As pastors know too well, speaking the truth without love often leads to harsh, cold legalism that drives congregations away. We all sin and fall short of the glory of God. Human imperfection has been around since the fall of man in Genesis 3; it's something we have to live with. We have to acknowledge it and sometimes ask forgiveness or accept punishment for our human errors. But we also have to remember that God knows we're fallible, and He forgives us. Even as sinners we can do great and good things through Christ Jesus.

On the other hand, speaking love without the truth leads to a liberalism that leaves people bereft of the true direction of God's Word. Yes, God is love; yes, Jesus consorted with every kind of low-life and forgave them. But Jesus never condoned sinful behavior. He never lowered His standards. Truth and love—the Christian story is a delicate balance of both. Pastors have to understand and maintain this balance.

People never get tired of a message that allows them to see, feel, and touch success. Point out those things in your church and community that are happening in a positive vein. Growing churches send out roots in every direction, so there are bound to be some encouraging results to highlight. Acknowledge the work members have done even when the rewards are meager. Especially if the rewards are meager. You want people to see and feel that they are part of a winning team, a thriving enterprise. Encourage people in their well doing.

At the same time, let them know that the task is not yet finished, that you have not yet become the church you need to be. Once you have some momentum going, that's no time to sit back and enjoy the show. Take a moment to celebrate God's goodness and then get back to work.

A New Point of View

To have an incredible growing church, leaders and members both have to have the right perspective. Unhealthy churches tend to foster a distorted image of themselves that inspires people to make wacky and often counterproductive decisions. The same problems may have been around for years, percolating to the surface from time to time then seeming to disappear before floating to the top again. Conflicts that everybody thought were resolved reemerge in new and ever more hostile forms. It's like looking at your church in a fun-house mirror; the image is hopelessly distorted because every time you move, it changes. Then when the set of variables you thought were accurate and based your decisions on turns out to be wrong, your plan of action falls apart. Your confidence fades. The congregation loses heart. New programs sputter to a halt. And the church keeps right on shrinking.

Some struggling churches hide their struggles like dirty family laundry. Everybody knows about the problems, but nobody is supposed to mention them. Or debate them. Or fix them. It's impossible to get a clear read on these seemingly invisible but very real issues, which makes it pretty much impossible to work through them. If you can't see what's wrong with a church, you can't form an accurate assessment of what's going on.

Someone once said that perspective is everything. While I think that's an overstatement, I know that attitude and perspective go a long way in determining a church's prospects for renewal. Looking at all the unknowns and half knowns in a church makes us afraid to act because, acting on inaccurate information, we might do the wrong thing. So there's an overwhelming fear of doing anything. Decision makers freeze up. The old ways might be wacky, but at least they're familiar and predictable.

How can you change all the negative circumstances that go into formulating your church perspective? You can't. But what you can do is not let them scare you. *Change your perspective.* Most of us spend a great deal of time trying to change circumstances and very little time changing perspective when the opposite may well be the best way to move forward. You can't change what the church has been, but you can change the way you look at it. I know many pastors who believe that if they could just change their churches their lives would be much better. I believe that our perspective in life has a lot more power to shape the future than our circumstances.

Here's a tall tale that illustrates the point. When a man in Macon, Georgia, came upon a wild dog attacking a young boy, he quickly grabbed the animal and throttled it with his two hands. A reporter saw the incident, congratulated the man, and told him his headline the following day would read, "Local Man Saves Child by Killing Vicious Animal."

The hero, however, told the journalist that he wasn't from Macon.

"Well, then," the reporter said, "the headline will probably say, 'Georgia Man Saves Child by Killing Dog.'"

"Actually," the man said, "I'm from Connecticut."

"In that case," the reporter said in a huff, "the headline will read, 'Yankee Kills Family Pet.'"[12]

A Perspective of Victory

Perspective is a great determiner in life. One place where it makes all the difference in the world is the area of spiritual victory. Church leaders need to rethink their perspective and look with expectation and assurance at how their church is going to experience spiritual victory. Fun-house images and fuzzy facts produce a perspective of fear, which leads to failure. The promises of the Bible replace that with a perspective of faith, which leads to success. This is one of the most important facts I have to share with you. Hold onto the promises of Scripture, ditch the fear, and forge ahead with faith.

Faith produces a vision for success that is impossible to capture if all you see is the mess your church has become. Remember all those variables we said we can't control? The idea of staking your future on them is enough to scare anybody. Irate members, a weak budget, neighborhood crime, a freeway running past your front door—you can't look ahead with joy and confidence if those kinds of things shape your perspective. Let faith shape your perspective. You haven't come to your calling as a pastor by accident. You haven't come to this church by accident. God is moving and working in your life, ready and willing for you to call on Him for assurance any time. Claim the faith that God has for you, base your perspective on faith instead of fear, and the Lord will show you the way to lead your church forward into a brighter future.

A perspective of faith is an effective pastor's indispensable ally. Along with it, there are other important characteristics that pastors cultivate in order to turn a church around. First on the list is *credibility*, both as a preacher and as a person. In his book *Preaching for Today*, Dr. Clyde Fant, former preacher, seminary professor, and dean of the chapel at Stetson University in Florida, defines *credibility* as "the weight given to the assertions of a speaker and the acceptance accorded him by his hearers." Credibility consists of two factors, trustworthiness and expertness; the greater the speaker's trustworthiness and expertness, the greater his credibility.[13]

You don't have to know everything to lead your church to new heights, but you do have to be reliable, credible, and base what you say on solid facts delivered with conviction. You can't do the job by merely dazzling the world with your impeccable stage presence while failing to love them as a pastor. We all know preachers who simultaneously display amazing factual confidence and pulpit polish along with unbelievable relational ignorance. This is a tough personality shortcoming to correct because it's a lot easier to reconsider your facts if they're in question than it is to rethink the way you relate to others after those nasty old habits become ingrained. You have to show experience and credibility; you have to be both reliable and trustworthy.

Be Trustworthy, Credible, Consistent

If a pastor loses his trustworthiness, he's finished. Pastors have to review their motivations regularly, looking deep into their hearts to ask why they do what they do. Is the pastor committed to selfless Christian service following in the footsteps of the Lord Jesus? If not, he should reconsider his vocation in the ministry. Trustworthiness and credibility are hot topics today when it comes to high-profile preachers on television and in the bookstores. There's nothing wrong with notoriety or material success as long as the prime objective is always to preach the Word and share the gospel. Remember those Christian ministers who have become media figures and have used their fame selflessly to lead the world to Christ. We can also think of high-visibility personalities who have turned out to be sham Christians, preaching a false or one-sided gospel on cable while exhorting their listeners to send them money, using it to buy mansions, private jets, and other expensive goodies that benefit them rather than the ministry. I've often thought if one day some viewers who had never heard of Christianity saw one of these

TV shows, they would think it was the silliest, most self-serving excuse for a religion that ever existed.

These are extreme examples, but the more subtle ones are actually far more common and more likely to trip up a well-meaning pastor. Does he seem to be pursuing ministry for monetary or professional gain? Does he seem to care for nothing beyond climbing the career ladder and boosting his star status? Is he constantly dropping the names of prominent figures he knows in order to build up his own reputation and sense of importance? If so, he's undermining his own trustworthiness and credibility for the sake of personal interest.

Credibility means you don't have to manipulate people to win them over. Of course debate and give-and-take in the marketplace of ideas are part of a pastor's stock in trade. Persuasion is not manipulation. Everyone in the Bible from Moses on down was involved in persuasion. Jesus delivered His parables as a form of persuasion as well as teaching. However, when motivation and methods become manipulative, you must look carefully at what is driving this desire for change.

Consistency is also part of what makes a pastor trustworthy. Inconsistency tends to be a sin of omission, often an unconscious one at that, and not a sin of commission. Many pastors may not be deliberately manipulative, nor are they self-centered, but they are careless with their facts. Sermon illustrations are a notorious area for inaccuracy and inconsistency. Unfortunately the phrase "preacher story" has become an idiom for an unbelievable assertion. If a story you want to use sounds unbelievable, either be able to document it or don't tell it! No one in society should have greater credibility than the man who speaks for Christ.

The Right Charisma, and Beyond

The word *charismatic* has all sorts of overtones to its meaning, some of them unflattering and even spooky. But in its proper context, charismatic is an accurate description for a good pastor. Every pastor needs to be seen as a charismatic individual. I'm not talking about the off-brand, wild-eyed, arm-waving pseudo-theologian. I'm talking about a charismatic public persona in the best and truest sense of the word.

A charismatic leader is possessed by a purpose greater than himself. He shows an enthusiasm for life, composure under stress, dedication to the goal, and an understanding and innovation that we see in the life of our Lord Jesus Christ. Everyone can learn to be more charismatic in these ways. Almost all pastors I know truly believe that the purpose they serve is greater than themselves.

Congregations feel that sincere charisma. It adds a passion, an electricity to every message that helps underscore its importance in the lives of the people. When you preach, exalt God's Word. Let the text do its wonderful work. Look people in the eye and tell them what God's Word says. Show the conviction you feel; let it come out in a sincere, genuine way. Take time to memorize Scripture passages and share them from your heart. Work hard on providing applications that speak to the people right where they are. Meet them at their point of comprehension, their point of need. This is not manipulation. This is the work of a leader who is truly charismatic because he is possessed by a purpose greater than himself. That purpose enhances his perspective of faith.

Pastors need to develop several more general skills in order to solidify a perspective of faith and help their churches break out of a slump. For one, as we've already seen, they need to hold fast to a long-term vision. Pastors have to be willing to stay put and see beyond the horizon of trouble. Too many ministers believe that the current crisis they're involved in (and there's normally at least one going on at any given time) is something they will never be able to get beyond. Pastors who are in it for the long haul are the ones who will bring their churches to a new level of growth and passion.

Pastors must also be confident in the possibilities of God. Is God actually able to bring a church to a new level of passion and growth?

Is our God truly able to do this? Pastors who are confident in God's power are able to take their churches through this transition.

Pastors have to be good at conflict management. I don't like conflict, but I've learned *never* to run from it. That only postpones the inevitable and often allows situations to become worse before you can deal with them. I can recall many instances in my last several churches where I have had to deal directly with conflict. This is never desirable or easy to do, but grabbing hold of the problem and solving it responsibly even if (especially if) it ruffles some feathers teaches lessons that reverberate through the church. It says we won't limp along with the status quo any more. We won't tiptoe around these giant, troublesome, divisive issues just because we've done so in the past. A healthy church doesn't shove conflict under the rug but deals with difficult situations deliberately and definitively.

There'll probably be some hurt feelings afterward, and you have to make sure those people don't feel alienated or that others have ganged up on them. Here is a key area for deacon involvement; involve your deacons and especially your deacon leadership in the process. Explain to them that a healthy church must deal with its problems lovingly, calmly, yet consistently and in accordance with Scripture. Let them know that disagreements will always be welcome but disagreeableness will not be tolerated.

The pastor also needs to be able to relate to subgroups within the church body and within the culture of the surrounding community. While naturally everyone will feel more at home with some groups than others, preachers must make a concentrated effort to relate effectively to every group within the congregation.

This outreach further encourages and promotes trust and openness of relationship. For example, on Wednesday evenings during our church suppers, I personally go to every table and speak to every person there. Even though there are hundreds of people present, I make a concerted effort to talk to and relate to every person in the congregation. I also believe that it is important to try to attend as many Sunday school functions as possible so that I can have more intimate spiritual relationships. If your church is small, go visit your members in their homes. If it's too big to do that, reach out to Sunday school classes, Bible studies, women's organizations, and other groups.

Pastors also need to spend time in prayer regarding their overall self-image. Those who lead breakthrough churches are confident in their call to the ministry. While everyone loves to be loved and deeply appreciates emotional strokes from their friends, the pastor who is able to make a true difference is confident in God's call even when emotional strokes are not forthcoming. You need to believe in who called you and what He called you to do. It is good to have affirmation, but it must not become what you seek first or most.

The Call

For most pastors the call to preach was one of the most dramatic, most intensely personal moments in life. The next time you feel beaten down and like you are out of ideas and out of gas spiritually, remember that day when God touched you in a special way and set you on the path to your life mission.

Many people have written inspiring accounts of their call to ministry, and the stories are as varied and individual as the people themselves. Chuck Colson, former advisor to President Richard Nixon and founder of Prison Fellowship, talks often about the night he spent sitting with his friend Tom Phillips on the screen porch of Phillips's home and having the Christian gospel sink in for the first time as Tom explained it. Colson was a ruthless political insider who had a well-deserved reputation as Nixon's hatchet man. But driving home later that evening, overcome with the magnitude of his sin and the joy of Christ's sacrifice, he started crying so hard he had to pull over because he couldn't see the road through his tears.

My good friend and colleague Jimmy Draper heard the call at an old-fashioned youth revival in Texas when he was fourteen. That hot August night he was praying silently for someone else when he felt God telling him to be a preacher. That wasn't what Jimmy had in mind, but then he felt the Lord saying, "How can I answer your prayer if you're not willing to do what I want you to do?" In that moment he stepped forward, walked down front as the music played, and surrendered to preach. "It's a mystical thing, like being saved," he recalled years later. "You feel God calling you to something different from the secular world, something of a spiritual nature. Baptists have a sense of calling you; it's a plan God has for your life, not a vocational choice you make. I surrendered any right I had to be anything else and vowed to devote myself to the work of the Lord."

In his classic autobiography, *Just As I Am*, Billy Graham shared the story of the night he felt God's call. He was in college at Florida Bible Institute and had already been preaching in youth groups and trailer parks, but he didn't feel at peace with the thought of a career in ministry. He started taking long walks on the school golf course at night,

> struggling with the Holy Spirit over the call of God to be a minister. That was the last thing I wanted to be, and I had used all kinds of rationalizations to convince God to let me do something else. . . .

But God wouldn't turn him loose, and after weeks of thinking it through, he began to see himself as a preacher.

> But did I want to preach for a lifetime? I asked myself that question for the umpteenth time on one of my nighttime walks around the golf course. The inner, irresistible urge would not subside. Finally, one night, I got down on my knees at the edge of one of the greens. Then I prostrated myself on the dewy turf. "O God," I sobbed, "if you want me to serve you, I will."

> The moonlight, the moss, the breeze, the green, the golf course—all the surroundings stayed the same. No sign in the heavens. No voice from above. But in my spirit I knew I had been called to the ministry. And I knew my answer was yes.[14]

My own call was not nearly so dramatic, but I remember it vividly and still draw strength from it every day.

Being raised in Greensboro, North Carolina, as the son of a foundry worker and seamstress, life was not always easy. There were times of economic hardship and uncertainty. Seeking a better future, my family had moved from my birthplace in Robbins, North Carolina, to Greensboro. There the family was uninvolved in church, but a wonderful family who lived nearby began to invite the children of our family to Sunday school and worship at a local Baptist church. As a young child I attended a Vacation Bible School. Back then part of the program was a commencement service that was a public time of encouragement to children. During that service I told everyone there that I was going to be a Baptist preacher when I grew up. Simply put, I have no conscious memory of anything other than God's wish for me to be a minister of the gospel.

Some have pointed out that mine is contrary to the experience of most. I certainly agree that it is. This is made even more poignant when you realize that I did not accept Christ until I was nine years of age.

Perhaps because of the uncertainties of home life and economic difficulties, I found the church to be a place of security, peace, and God's love. My young heart responded to God's call at an early age. This call was encouraged by a positive experience in the local church. I loved to be a part of God's family. Even prior to my salvation, I would find rides to church and was eager to be involved in the various goings-on. In fact, the night of my salvation, I was there by myself on a Sunday evening. But I wasn't alone for long. My family later came to Christ as well. In those days I would also find ways to go out on evangelistic visitation with older men in the church. I was too frightened to say anything but was delighted to see them share

Christ with others. It affected me deeply and helped me understand the need to be a soul winner, a witness for Christ.

My young years were not always the picture that some would wish for their childhood. However, I must thank God that He reached out to me and provided a church where I could hear the Word of God, grow in Him, and learn the skills I needed.

The Bible gives us some wonderful commentary on the call to preach. In his letter to the Ephesians, Paul wrote, "I, therefore, the prisoner of the Lord, urge you to walk worthy of the calling you have received, with all humility and gentleness, with patience, accepting one another in love, diligently keeping the unity of the Spirit with the peace that binds us. There is one body and one Spirit, just as you were called to one hope at your calling; one Lord, one faith, one baptism, one God and Father of all, who is above all and through all and in all" (4:1–6).

The Holman Bible Handbook adds:

> Ephesians is the perfect balance between doctrine and duty. . . . We learn from Paul's balanced perspective the need for both orthodoxy (right belief) and orthoproxy (right living). Commentators have suggested that the pivotal verse of the entire letter—indeed, the key that unlocks its structure—is 4:1. . . . The church's privileged position and calling carries with it weighty responsibilities. Paul exhorted the church to worthy living. He emphasized the character and effort required for such exemplary living (4:1–3). Then with characteristic Trinitarian emphasis the apostle claimed the church could so live because it is energized by the Spirit, established by the Lord, and empowered by the Father.[15]

Preachers with the sense of calling, the perspective and purpose that Paul describes, are the leaders that churches have to have in order to thrive. They're the ones who can carry a congregation through the exciting and sometimes rocky transformation from mediocre to magnificent.

The Big Explosion

Eventually, effective church leaders assemble all the components they need to reinvigorate their congregations and move from the talk-and-theory stage into the action mode. It's like in an old movie when the scientist has all his smoking flasks and beakers around him, the sparking generators are at full power, and he finally pours all his bubbling ingredients together and pulls the switch. Kaboom! It's the big explosion, the moment of truth, the tipping point, when all the plans are set in motion and the big change begins: the shrinking is reversed. In *Breakout Churches,* Thom Rainer describes this moment as the "chrysalis factor," when all the components of a successful turnaround reach critical mass and the church changes direction from downward-trending to upward growth. It's an exciting and dynamic time when the church finally pulls out of its death spiral and starts to climb again.[16]

Rainer, Jim Collins (in his book *Good to Great*), and many other experts talk about the moment in the life of a transitioning church or other organization when everything starts to jell. Sometimes it's a cataclysmic moment like the laboratory blowup; and other times it's a more gradual, step-by-step process that leads to greatness. Collins and others underscore the fact that just being good isn't good enough when you can be great at what you do.

Part of the motivation for pastors to help their churches grow is this notion that, when it comes to communities of Christian faith, just being good sells God short. He deserves the best we can offer. Collins begins his best-selling book with the statement, "Good is the enemy of great."[17] He's right. A church that's just getting by, not losing lots of members but not really going anywhere spiritually, should be an embarrassment to Christians everywhere. Rainer refers to Jesus' charge to believers down through the ages at the end of the book of Matthew quoted before: "Go, therefore, and make disciples of all nations, baptizing them in the name of the Father and of the Son and of the Holy Spirit, teaching them to observe everything I have commanded you. And remember, I am with you always, to the end of the age" (Matt. 28:19–20). Dr. Rainer reminds us that this isn't called the Good Commission but the Great Commission.

The imagery of Thom Rainer's "chrysalis factor" is right on target. Before its mysterious transformation into a beautiful butterfly, a caterpillar spins a little chamber called a chrysalis around itself that hides all the transformational steps from view. It goes in a fuzzy bug and comes out a brilliant flying marvel. This process is a wonder of God's creation. Pastors can lead churches through the chrysalis stage to a grand transformation of their own. The people look around one day and say, "What is happening all of a sudden that wasn't happening before?"

What takes place in the chrysalis stage of a church in transition? No two churches are exactly the same. The breakout churches that Rainer and his research team studied didn't have any of the obvious characteristics you might assume they would have. The pastor wasn't necessarily a bold, flashy, outwardly dynamic leader; the church wasn't an early adapter of trends or methods; there wasn't a splashy vision statement that everybody rallied around. But what there was in every case was a leader dedicated to biblical leadership principles who had a vision for growth.

Rainer observes, "The leaders of breakout churches did not devise some elaborate process to discover vision. Most of them did not initially have a vision to share with others. To the contrary, as one breakout church leader commented, 'Vision discovered me.' The researchers found that the leaders discovered vision through intersection of three factors: the passion of the leader; the needs of the community; and the gifts, abilities, talents, and passions of the congregation."[18]

He points out the leadership model in the book of Acts, written by Jesus' apostle Luke, who says in the first chapter that Christians (and I believe leaders in particular) have to be led by the Holy Spirit. Luke records the words of Jesus: "It is not for you to know times or periods that the Father has set by His own authority. But you will receive power when the Holy Spirit has come upon you, and you will be My witnesses in Jerusalem, in all Judea and Samaria, and to the ends of the earth" (Acts 1:7–8).

Legacy Leadership

Following the story line of Acts, Rainer identifies various stages of leadership development, ending with what he calls Acts 6/7 Legacy Leadership. In Acts 6, the twelve apostles need help fulfilling their growing obligations and appoint seven men to distribute food to widows on their behalf. The Twelve stick with their praying and preaching, equipping others to serve publicly in the name of Christ while staying behind the scenes themselves. It's a great instance of servant leadership following the example of Christ. Luke adds, "The proposal pleased the whole company" (Acts 6:5).

Acts 7 recounts the testimony of Stephen, one of the seven chosen in chapter 6, who was falsely accused of blasphemy and brought before the Sanhedrin, the high Jewish council under Roman oversight that harassed and threatened Jesus' followers because their message threatened the Sanhedrin's power and influence. Stephen was a visionary who saw his place in the big picture of church history and focused on the future of the church rather than the present. His statements and decisions were for the benefit of the church's long-term health, lifting up others, shying away from the spotlight, yet ready to assume responsibility for things gone wrong. Stephen boldly recounted the story of the house of Abraham being driven by famine into Egypt, Moses leading the people back to the promised land in fulfillment of prophecy, Israel's rebellion, and King Solomon's magnificent temple.

In conclusion he declared, "You stiff-necked people with uncircumcised hearts and ears! You are always resisting the Holy Spirit; as your forefathers did, so do you. . . . You received the law under the direction of angels and yet have not kept it" (7:51, 53).

Stephen was a bold visionary who saw the whole sweep of church history. He was a powerful voice for truth and spoke up without hesitation even under hostile circumstances. He would probably have made a great leader of a comeback church today. But in his time and place, Stephen served God in another way. His attitude cost him his life: the same day he stood up to the Sanhedrin, he became the Christian church's first martyr. Obviously today's leaders aren't asked to make that level of sacrifice, but Stephen's example shows the stuff leaders are made of. If you want a backbone to model yours after, his is the one. He was the embodiment of passionate leadership, the kind of leader who can carry a church through the chrysalis stage.

The Third Rail

Politicians sometimes refer to a controversial matter as a third-rail issue. The expression comes from the center rail of electric commuter trains, which carry a deadly charge. If you touch it, you're cooked; and that's what happens if you bring up a volatile third-rail subject in the political arena: just mentioning it makes sparks fly because it's so divisive. As a church leader I've learned that proposing changes in the worship service is often the ultimate third-rail challenge. Yet it's also often a core component of the chrysalis factor, one of those big components that comes out transformed.

Do you face resistance in your church to changes that you feel sure would help you grow? Is your caterpillar doomed before it can turn into a butterfly? For your church to have a chance of moving forward, do you have to grab the third rail? You may have to take that risk! Stephen surely would have done it. Pastors with a perspective of faith have to be willing to break out of old paths and old ways of doing things if they're no longer fruitful and try something new, even if it involves personal risk. Changing the old routine will likely cause problems because no matter how hopelessly ineffective something is, a group of people will hang onto it. It's always worked in the past, and besides it was Mrs. Jones's favorite part of the church, and we all know how dedicated to the Lord's work Mrs. Jones was.

In the last fifty years or so, Christian churches have revisited their worship services with dramatic, even historic results. The Catholic Church broke with centuries of tradition by holding services in the language of worshippers around the world rather than in Latin. American Protestant churches, which had used a more or less consistent worship format since the early 1800s, began to broaden their thinking about the Sunday morning church experience after World War II. During the 1960s congregations experimented with folk services, new kinds of music, and informal settings. Some of these efforts clearly went too far, crossing the boundary of respectful behavior. (I heard the story of a Sunday morning chapel service during the 1970s at a prestigious private university where the minister used champagne for communion, saying "Cheers!" as he popped the cork to "celebrate Jesus.")

When I came to Taylors First Baptist Church, I believed that one of the things necessary for our church to stop shrinking was to stop planning services like it was 1955 and everybody still wore hats. We had to start a new, more contemporary service that would relate to the large segment of our church that had been leaving in droves. When I shared my vision for this type of service with members of the church, I told them that I was not willing to lose a generation of young people and young adults to this world because we didn't offer them a worship experience where they felt at home.

The next Wednesday night an older gentlemen came up to me and confessed his objection to a contemporary service until he heard me say what I said about losing a generation. Then he said, "Pastor, while I may not attend that service or even like the music in that service, count me in as one who supports our desire to reach a generation for Christ." He was willing to break out of a rut. He was humble enough to admit he didn't have all the answers and that he was willing to go along with a change that would benefit the body of Christ even if he personally didn't like it. Churches have to be willing to do that. Otherwise the shrinking continues.

As we've already seen, the music you perform in church sets the mood for the service more than anything else. Rick Warren calls music "one of the most critical (and controversial) decisions you make in the life of your church."[19] If your church was founded more than fifty years ago, the original members probably didn't give much thought to the music because your denomination used certain music and that was that. Electric guitars? Drums? Hand mikes? Plexiglas pulpits? No pulpits? These questions never came up then. Now they can start a fistfight.

Explain to everybody that it's OK to prefer one style of music but not to equate their style with God's style. Probably some members will embrace change with a hearty "At last!" while others will fight it tooth and nail, insisting the church hang onto the great traditions of the past. It's likely that by "great traditions" they mean the music of the late nineteenth and early twentieth centuries—pieces like "Just As I Am," "How Great Thou Art," "Standing on the Promises," and so forth. These are great, timeless hymns; and they have their place in worship even today. But they can't shoulder the load on their own.

And speaking of great traditions, what about Mozart and Haydn in the 1700s or Palestrina in the Renaissance? What about Gregorian chant? How far back should we go in the name of tradition? To the psalms of David? We know that at least some of them were written to be set to music, but since there was no system to write down or record music at the time, we have no idea what it sounded like. Visionary church leaders have to attack musical and worship snobbery and let people know that God can be worshipped in a variety of ways and settings. As long as the Word is being preached and integrity is a common factor in worship planning and presentation, they should be willing to support whatever a church does to reach out.

In our church we chose to leave a rather traditional service for those who prefer it. We have not tried to change anybody's preferences for one musical style over another. I don't think we could do it anyway. So we have two services, one leaning to the more traditional format and one more contemporary. The contemporary service has hundreds more people every week than the traditional one, but both of them help the church do its work.

Whether your pulpit is pine or Plexiglas is a lot less important than what the pastor says when he's standing behind it. Whether your music is the stately tones of a magnificent pipe organ or the enthusiastic beat of a guitar combo, the essential thing is what the lyrics say and how well they nurture the spirit of those who hear it.

First Matters

Leaders also know that innovative programming, new worship styles, and all these other changes aren't in themselves solutions to low growth. Rather they're the tools church leaders use to define the direction of change and complete a transition faster. In the hands of diligent, praying, God-directed people, they can work incredible changes. These leaders identify and describe problems—even longstanding ones—face them honestly, and have the faith and confidence to lead toward a solution. The sight of roadblocks in the pathway ahead don't faze them; they only energize them to call on their faith with greater confidence.

You have to follow up a vision for growth with strategic planning to translate it into action. Bold leaders have a vision for an effective worship experience and the ability to impart that vision to others. Give your church a specific road map for getting the church from where it is to where it needs to be. Our church is currently in the middle of a strategic initiative called First Matters. This is an attempt to revitalize our programs in the areas of prayer, communication, evangelism, discipleship, missions, and stewardship. Several years ago when I came to this particular church, we spent months studying God's purposes for the church as well as developing a recognizable and communicable vision statement. What we ended up with is: "We are here to love the Lord as we lead others to the same love."

This statement is constantly placed before the congregation in all our publications and media outlets. It's human nature for people to forget what you tell them. So with something as fundamental and important as this, we have to keep reminding them of it. It's our version of Rick Warren's "recasting the vision." There are First Matters posters everywhere and regular updates on what we are doing in each program area. Staff members are assigned responsibility to make sure every part of their organization pulls together in these strategic initiatives.

First Matters was founded on one of Jesus' lessons from the Sermon on the Mount: "Don't worry about your life, what you will eat or what you will drink; or about your body, what you will wear. . . . Learn how the wildflowers of the field grow: they don't labor or spin thread. Yet I tell you that not even Solomon in all his splendor was adorned like one of these! . . . So don't worry, saying, 'What will we eat?' . . . or 'What will we wear?' . . . But seek first the kingdom of God and His righteousness, and all these things will be provided for you" (Matt. 6:25, 28–29, 31, 33). The objective of First Matters was to seek God's will as we planned changes at our church in order to turn it around.

I said over and over that while the *methods* we used to present the gospel needed to change, our *message* must never change. First Matters was the product of six hard-working subcommittees, each analyzing the need for change in a specific area. As these committees were forming their plans, we got word out to the congregation about the new ministries and new approaches they were developing. I was careful to temper the excitement (or apprehension) of the process with a reminder that all these changes wouldn't be happening at once, nor would everything be done by the church staff. I think there's an expectation that whenever something in church needs doing the staff will take care of it one way or another. This isn't a healthy attitude, and it doesn't happen in our church. These dreams, I explained, would be lay driven and staff guided; we would all work together to see God do great things.

For each of the six areas of concentration, we began with a foundation of Scripture, then presented a statement of what we felt God calling our church to do in that area. Following that was a bullet-point strategy for translating that call into action on our part. I won't unfold the whole program here, but, for example, under missions our heading was "Missions Matter at Taylors First Baptist."

The biblical bedrock of this affirmation is in the Great Commission of Matthew 28 and Jesus' comment in Acts 1 that power comes in the wake of the Holy Spirit. We also find in Paul's explanation to the Ephesians that God equips His people differently to share the gospel in different parts of His kingdom: "He personally gave some to be apostles, some prophets, some evangelists, some pastors and teachers, for the training of the saints in the work of ministry, to build up the body of Christ, until we all reach unity in the faith and in the knowledge of God's son" (Eph. 4:11–12).

From this Scripture came the following vision statement: "We believe that God has given each one of us as believers a biblical mandate to be on mission with Him." The strategy for carrying out vision, based on those Scriptures, was then distilled into a series of concise, specific bullets. Some of them were:

- Each church member actively participates in an area of missions each year.
- Organize our missions ministry into four areas—local, state, national, and international, and seek to better equip and educate our members to understand and follow God's call for each of us to be on mission with God.
- Become a multiplying church by planting a church each year among different ethnic groups or in different geographical areas, in order to reach the various segments of the greater Greenville community for Christ.
- Create a Missions Mobilization Center for equipping and mobilizing teams, informing members of opportunities, and increasing overall missions awareness.
- Partner with other Great Commission churches and organizations to win others for Christ in our community and around the world.

Throughout the process of developing and implementing First Matters, we set high standards. It's better not to do anything at all than to launch some sort of initiative in a halfhearted way. We work with an expectation of excellence and an expectation of success in every phase of the program. Nobody wants to join in a project if it's lackluster or has a self-defeating air about it, but everybody wants to be part of a dynamic, enthusiastic, on-fire outreach. Effective leaders help people catch the vision for something new.

First Matters works because it offers a way for everybody to get involved; the pastors, staff, and congregation all have responsibilities, and everyone is invested in the process and its outcome. If it were a program the leaders carried out alone, it wouldn't attract nearly the interest or have anything like the support it enjoys today. When a church is finally moving toward a chrysalis factor transformation or taking best advantage of the Big Kaboom, church leaders can't do all the work by themselves. It takes a congregation to shrink a church, and it takes a congregation to unshrink one.

The Right People on the Bus

However dedicated you are, however much faith you claim, you're not going to be able to rescue a shrinking church by yourself. You have to have the right colaborers around to help you do it, men and women who share your vision for growth and believe in it as passionately as you do. While there's no silver bullet for turning around a troubled church, having the right team for the task is a powerful tool.

We've all heard stories about the bold leader who stepped out in confidence, then looked back to see everybody else behind him—*way* behind him! Studies of churches and other organizations are full of warnings about the importance of having a team that shares enthusiasm and commitment during a season of change. In *Breakout Churches,* Thom Rainer underscores the importance of "getting the right people on board"[20] early in the process. Then at some point a sense of momentum takes hold, and there's an exhilarating feeling that the bad old days are finally behind you. The Big Kaboom worked. This promising new reality comes from a combination of your own faith vision, the contribution of church staff, and the groundswell of support from lay leaders and other church members. Once that can-do feeling pushes out the stale defeatism of the past and establishes itself as the new norm, people catch the sense of excitement and start pitching in because they want to be part of a winning team.

As Rainer notes, once the balance started to tip in favor of change in the churches he studied, "The men and women who began filling places of ministry were motivated to do the work to which God had called them for his glory. The right people led the transformation of the church from an environment of mediocrity to an environment of excellence. This environment of excellence in turn attracted more of the right people."

It's one of those chicken-and-egg questions: "Will the right people be attracted to the church because of its culture of excellence, or is that culture a result of having the right people on board?"

People of Excellence

Hiring the right person for a particular job or choosing the right volunteer for a key position is one of the most important, frustrating, mine field-encrusted, difficult processes on earth for a pastor. Many thousands of words have been written about the dynamic relationship between staff and leadership, the pitfalls of hiring and firing, and everything else associated with this process. Nevertheless, it's still a highly mysterious and treacherous path. Dr. Rainer writes, "Very few leaders are satisfied with the process of finding the right person, and even fewer are satisfied that they found the right persons, for paid or volunteer positions."

The main reasons for this are both obvious and hard to avoid. Some are a challenge in any organization, and others are particular to churches, which have an extra layer of politics and personalities that other places don't. For example, both paid and volunteer workers may also be members of the congregation, sometimes part of an extended family with long-standing ties to the church. If they're not right for the job, what do you do? Fire one of your own members? Work around them? You can be sure that whatever you do, somebody's going to be unhappy.

The good news is that once the winds of change begin to blow, you'll suddenly find it easier to attract what Rainer calls "people of excellence" to join you. "The reasons are twofold," he explains.

> First, these churches tend to attract the best people because of their clear and compelling vision. Second, the breakout church leaders often do not wait for an opening before bringing a person on staff or providing a place for a lay leader to serve. If they come across a promising individual, they invite him or her to join the team even if there is no clear place for the person at the time. It typically does not take long before that capable and motivated person is making a difference in the church using his or her God-given gifts and abilities. Within a short time of becoming aware of the great need for the church to make significant changes, the leaders were pursuing both the right people and the right infrastructure.[21]

He quotes a metaphor Jim Collins uses in *Good to Great* that I think paints a wonderful image of what a leader aims for when he's assembling, or reassembling, his staff: "The right people on the bus, the wrong people off the bus, and the right people in the right seats."[22]

A fascinating corollary to this picture is that in Collins's research leaders who led the charge for positive change didn't first pick a destination, map out their route, and decide what they'd do when they got there. They didn't worry about where the bus was going. They got the right people on the bus and the wrong people off the bus, then figured out which direction to head.

Reality Check

That's not usually what happens in real life. Churches tend to follow what Rainer calls the "traditional and often unsuccessful formula for finding staff" by sticking with the same job description as the person who left and hiring the first decent prospect who comes through the door. "Mrs. Smith is leaving as secretary. We've got to find a new secretary!" "John is resigning as youth pastor. We've got to get another youth pastor in here pronto!" Do we need a new secretary? A new youth pastor? Could we make better use of our resources and be a better church by building a staff for the future that is different from the staff of the past? Nobody stops to ask those questions. It may also be that no one considers whether the new hire is personally compatible with the current staff. "Personal chemistry" is subjective, but when it's bad, it makes life miserable for everybody.

Weak churches shy away from increasing the size of the staff; they can't imagine adding a person unless there is an official vacancy. They wouldn't dream of hiring some creative, dynamic individual on the basis of potential benefit to the church and figuring out later what his responsibilities would be. They never think about hiring someone for a newly created position based on anticipated needs or adding staff ahead of the growth curve. They don't take the initiative; they only react. They conduct business as usual, Rainer notes, "and as a result, stay on the path of slow erosion."

Three Steps to Smart Staffing

Jim Collins and other researches summarize their advice about staff in three sentences: (1) When in doubt about a prospective staff addition, don't hire anybody. (2) When you need to fire someone, do it decisively and soon. (3) Put your best people on your biggest opportunities, not your biggest problems. Rainer goes on to discuss two of these suggestions in detail.

When in doubt about a hiring decision, wait. Churches often learn this lesson the hard way, stacking up horror tales of filling a slot as quickly as possible only to produce disastrous results. It's better to have an unfilled position, giving someone else the job temporarily or dividing it up among the remaining staffers, than to fill it with the wrong person.

In one illustration a pastor had been serving at a church two years when the associate pastor left. "Leaders in the church said we needed to fill the position because the church always had an associate pastor," the senior pastor reported. "I never really questioned if we needed an associate pastor or what the best job description for one might be."

When a church member told the pastor she knew a "fine man who has just been down on his luck," the pastor reacted instinctively and got the church's approval to hire him for the newly opened slot.

"It was a disaster waiting to happen," the pastor lamented. "I called his former church (where he had abruptly resigned), and their pastor told me he was just not a good fit, although he was a fine man. That should have sent bells ringing in my head. If he is such a fine man, why did the pastor recommend him to our church instead of keeping him at his church?

"It took me about three weeks to learn why he was not a good fit in the other church. He was a lazy bum! And he never did any of the things on his job description. All he wanted to do was counsel people. That's where he got his ego fulfillment. But counseling was not supposed to be part of his job description."

So what do you do now? It's likely to take far longer to get rid of a hiring mismatch than it did to bring him on in the first place. If the church had used that time to consider carefully both the job description and the applicants, it would have saved a lot of grief for everybody concerned. Now the church was in the uncomfortable position of trying to rid themselves of the person they'd just hired.

"Our response was like most churches," the pastor continued. "We did nothing. Oh we talked about it, fussed about it, and met about it. But we still did nothing. We just didn't want to deal with the conflict we knew we would have. I guess we thought we would have some kind of magical solution when we woke up one morning."

But of course the situation deteriorated instead. The associate pastor still did not do his basic assignments, and he spent more and more time counseling despite the fact that his job description did not mention counseling.

"By the time we decided we had to do something, we had a real mess. The associate pastor had built quite a following with his counselees and their families. When we made the painful decision to terminate him, we lost many families. I'll bet it took us two years to recover from that fiasco."[23]

However ill-suited someone is for the job, he'll always attract a following. Moving a misfit aside against his will, as this pastor's experience shows, typically alienates his supporters, who then square off against other members they see as the enemy. Sometimes the rift is severe enough that families will leave the church over it. All because an overeager church leadership was too quick to fill an open spot without carefully considering the job and the applicant in light of future needs, not present expediency.

Making Room for the Right Team

So what do you do if all at once you look around and notice that your team just isn't working? Once you've sized up the passenger list, how do you escort the wrong people off the bus to make room for the right ones with a minimum of commotion? As painful as it is, once you see what needs to be done, it's best to do it as quickly as possible. The more you draw out the process, the more distracting it is, and the more momentum and focus you lose. As Collins expressed it, "To let people languish in uncertainty for months or years, stealing precious time in their lives that they could use to move on to something else, when in the end they aren't going to make it anyway—*that* would be ruthless. To deal with it up front and let people get on with their lives—that is *rigorous*."

In the case of lay positions, if it isn't an important position, don't lose any sleep over it. Let the jobholder stay on the job for the sake of harmony and work around him in as unobtrusive a way as possible. However, if the person is in a key or influential position, you've got to change the situation. The cost is often high, but the cost of doing nothing is greater. Act quickly but with a Christian sense of propriety and sensitivity. Rainer proposes the steps of closure, compassion, and communication.

Pray about your decision and get a firm sense that it's the step God wants you to make for the good of His church. Once you're sure, tell the person in private what you've decided and why. Don't beat around the bush, don't apologize, don't argue. Make clear this is a done deal and is for the long-term benefit of all parties.

Expect criticism or anger toward your decision and accept it with compassion. Being fired is a major bump in the road in anyone's life. Financial security, social position, and self-image all take a serious hit. Justified as it is, terminating someone's job creates a lot of problems, and a compassionate leader listens humbly to whatever response there is. It's also important to extend the Christian hand of liberality. Offer a meaningful severance package, counseling, job placement assistance, and whatever else you can to help ease the transition.

Nothing revs up the rumor mill like someone getting fired. Be sure to announce the action officially. Keep personal information to a minimum, but get the truth out there so wild stories won't fill up the information vacuum.

Leaders for the Future

In addition to building a strong leadership team, pastors of growing churches also recognize the importance of training future leaders. In their book *Comeback Churches*, Ed Stetzer and Mike Dodson lift up the example of Pastor Richard Jueckstock of Willard Christian Alliance Church in Willard, Ohio, who emphasizes the priority of developing leaders. Members of his staff have been specifically assigned to nurture leaders in different areas of the church to multiply the effectiveness of a single insightful and inspired leadership vision. "One leader has worked to mentor and develop other small-group leaders; another trains evangelism teams. Some key leaders have decided they are going to be true disciples of Christ and have really studied the Scriptures."

In order to keep up the new direction and momentum, great leaders have to raise up others to carry on beyond the scope of what they themselves can do. This is one of the trickiest aspects of all when it comes to reviving a church. Getting that visionary leader is one big step, followed by building a team and inspiring the membership. But one person can't do it alone forever. Stetzer and Dodson write, "It is sad but true that many people who are 'take charge leaders' do not know how to replicate themselves. Leaders who cannot reproduce can lead a squad, but never an army." Replicating leaders are those who find resources to help them "intentionally develop leaders for the purpose of evangelistic growth." Leaders of leaders find ways to multiply themselves. "Godly leaders are just gifts from God to bring people to godly action."[24]

Finding Who Goes Where

Folded in with these other attributes is the importance of helping others find their best place of service in the church. In other words, once all the right people are on the bus, what do they do? Who's the best prospect for every necessary job? Gary L. McIntosh examines that question in *Biblical Church Growth*. He observes that churches need a "workable system to help people identify and use their spiritual gifts. The challenge is that the leaders are mostly volunteers and church must care for the same people it uses in ministry." "Churches that experience biblical church growth systematically recruit, train, and deploy members in ministry. Declining churches rarely have any defined system to identify potential volunteers, assess their giftedness, and place them in appropriate ministry positions."

Also, McIntosh adds, "Growing churches involve people early on in ministry. When Paul planted churches, he involved people in ministry quickly. Many times the people were inexperienced, but they were energetic and willing to serve." He did not wait to involve them until they were experts in something because by then they might lose interest or passion for the task, or be busy with something else. "Unless people become involved in ministry within three to six months after they first attend church on a regular basis," McIntosh reports, "they may never become involved." He continues,

> The mobilization of people to participate in direct service to each other and the world is a major ingredient in biblical church growth. The early church, described in Acts, grew not because growth was easy but because men and women committed themselves to sacrificial service to each other and to lost people. Filled with intense conviction, the power of the Holy Spirit, and love for God, ordinary men and women overcame tremendous obstacles to tell others about the Savior. Churches that effectively recruit, train, and deploy their people in faithful ministry will find they too have tremendous potential for biblical church growth.[25]

I'm reminded of the famous passage in Matthew 16:24–25 that lays out the challenge to all who would truly commit their lives to Christ. Speaking to His disciples, Jesus said, "If anyone wants to come with Me, he must deny himself, take up his cross, and follow Me. For whoever wants to save his life will lose it, but whoever loses his life because of Me will find it." Leaders have to convey that level of commitment and focus to the work of the church. That's not to say that every volunteer dishwasher or Sunday school teacher has to be prepared to die on the spot, but this is the level of keen spiritual commitment that underlies every task performed in the name of Jesus.

Time and again God has honored that commitment by renewing His church. Howard Snyder, writing in *Evaluating the Church*

Growth Movement, said, "It is God's will not only to plant, grow, and perfect the church but also to renew it.

> The Holy Spirit is both the creating Spirit and the renewing Spirit. "In the beginning," at Creation, "was the Word . . . through [whom] all things were made" (John 1:1–3 NIV), and the Word still brings "times of refreshing" (Acts 3:19 NIV) when God's people turn to him. The Bible, in both Testaments, is full of the language of renewal and new life. God is in the church renewal business. If we miss this renewal perspective, we too easily become impatient with stagnant, non-growing churches and put all the emphasis on starting new churches or "replanting" old ones. God wants to renew the church—*every* church—that will pay the price. And simply as a matter of strategy, effective church renewal can contribute at least as much to overall growth as can a focus on new church planting.[26]

Never Too Late

For an unforgettable example of God's power to renew us, we don't have to go any further than the otherworldly story in Ezekiel 37. The prophet Ezekiel is in a valley full of dry bones. And what he sees is an Old Testament miracle. "This is what the Lord GOD says to these bones: I will cause breath to enter you and you will live. I will put tendons on you, make flesh grow on you, and cover you with skin. I will put breath in you so that you come to life. Then you will know I am the LORD" (vv. 5–6). Ezekiel heard a rattling sound as the bones started to move and came together, bone on bone. Tendons, flesh, and skin formed to cover them. Then God breathed the breath of life into them and they "stood on their feet, a vast army" (v. 10).

Those dry bones could represent any struggling church about to shrink out of sight. The story is an encouraging reminder that no situation is hopeless where God is involved.

In his vision Ezekiel saw a change from dead bones to bones with living flesh on them that came together and formed a great army. If things had gone along the way they had in the past, the dry bones would have remained dry bones. Change was frightening at first to Ezekiel, and it's frightening to churches today as well. Those among the declining/plateaued group tend toward continuity rather than intentional change. Many drift aimlessly with little internal guidance. Even though they may be busy doing many good things, they are not engaged in the essentials of growth.

Churches that are breakout churches most often have long-range and short-range plans for their church. Again, lead your church to study about its reason for being. Organize the leaders of the church, committees, deacons, and so forth to gather data on the church and its community. Present the church with specific, attainable, and measurable goals that serve as a measuring stick for the success of the strategic plan. Earn the people's confidence and demonstrate that you have a plan of action with some energy and pizzazz and a high probability that the end result will be better than where you started. Teach them thoroughly and patiently. Do your homework and help them do theirs.

We've said that all growing churches share certain attributes. We've also said that no two churches have the same turnaround strategy and that you can't copy somebody else's growth plans and expect the same results. It would be nice to have a checklist titled "The Absolutely Foolproof Antidote for Your Incredible Shrinking Church" that you could run down, marking off the steps like a science experiment, and get a guaranteed result at the end. There are too many variables for this approach to work.

What you can do, however, is get ideas, inspiration, and encouragement from the examples of other churches that have run off the rails and somehow gotten back on track. Big or small, in metropolitan areas or rural locations, they each have a lesson to teach us. Let's see what we can learn from some of them.

Role Models

With all the information available on churches that have broken out of slumps, some of them steep and lasting for years, there's no need completely to reinvent the wheel. Though your specific problem set will be unique, you can still gather plenty of useful nuggets from churches that have been down the revitalization road ahead of you. It's important to recognize the need to disciple your leaders in the attitudes of church growth. Take yourself, your staff, and your lay leaders through some of the many excellent studies of breakthrough churches. Read and discuss books such as *The Purpose Driven Church*. And you can take steps to enhance the atmosphere for taking a new approach. Set up team building and idea building exercises. Conduct a prayer retreat and ask God humbly and sincerely what He wants for your church. Lead your members to set specific and attainable goals and again reward them through public recognition for their accomplishments. Tell them what God wants for the church.

Effective leaders of renewed churches don't act on the basis of what they personally want to do, or who shouts the loudest or contributes the most money. They pray, plan, and learn from churches that have gone before. We've looked briefly at a number of them already, but let's take a few minutes to examine a few more in greater detail. They represent every kind of challenge a struggling church can face. Sometimes the response seems absolutely radical, but it worked. That's not to say the same solution would do the job in your case. The idea here is not to say this is what you ought to do but rather that this is an innovative way to approach the problem of a shrinking church. Don't copy the examples verbatim, but copy the innovation and confidence you see. Look at how these churches think outside the box. See how they acknowledge that there's a problem and then get going to find the answer with humility and enthusiasm. These examples will give you hope for the future of your church, whatever shape it's in.

Comeback Churches touches on the stories of more than three hundred turn-around congregations of every size across the country. One of them is Homestead Heights Baptist Church in Durham, North Carolina. Homestead Heights was a large, old church that faced trouble on the outside and on the inside. The neighborhood was changing around them, and political turmoil sapped their energy from within. A few years ago the youth pastor there, J. D. Greear, was called to be the senior pastor and lead the church "in a fresh direction."[27]

From Homestead to High School

It was a fresh direction all right, beginning with the name change from Homestead Heights Baptist to Summit Church. The church recommitted itself to becoming "intentionally missional." By that the authors mean a church that

> responds to the commands of Jesus by becoming incarnational, indigenous, and intentional in its context. When Jesus said, "As the Father has sent Me, I also send you" (John 20:21), the mandate was not for a select group of cross-cultural missionaries. It was a commission to you, to me, and to our churches. We have a sender (Jesus), a message (the gospel), and a people to whom we are sent (those in our

> culture). It is worth the effort to go beyond personal preferences and attractional methods to proclaim the gospel in our church services and outside the walls.[28]

Summit Church definitely went beyond personal preferences and methods. They sold their historic building and moved into a high school! "This approach seems backward to many traditional churches, but Summit Church considers it a great opportunity to become mobile and find a location that better suits their mission. Their once-dwindling attendance [in the 600s] now tops 1,600 and is still growing."

The 400 Percent Solution

Peniel Baptist Church in rural Palatka, Florida, had about 125 attending on an average Sunday, a figure they'd been stuck at for years. Then they called Danny Williams as their pastor. He had a vision for change, the ability to communicate his vision, and the energy to lead the way. Under Danny's leadership, the church "began a process of reorganization—from Sunday school to leader training, to prayer and outreach. Lay leaders embraced and increased the vision. They contacted every missing member (hundreds were on the rolls but had not attended for some time). They implemented a church-wide prayer ministry. Finally, they decided to get directly involved in church planting, helping start a church in Crescent Beach, Florida."[29] In eight years, average attendance increased 400 percent to five hundred per week. One of those years they baptized more than a hundred people.

Harvest Twelve

One surprise that can spoil a promising comeback plan is if new members are coming in the front door but nobody notices the hoards slipping out the back. These churches add members to the rolls but lose existing members just as fast or faster. Pastor George Stevenson at East Gate Church of the Nazarene in Roanoke, Virginia, developed what he called the Harvest Twelve ministry, combining what he considered to be the dozen most important ministries in the church, then signing up a hundred laymen to concentrate on that list.

New Member Boot Camp

Lots of troubled churches make the mistake of resorting to gimmicks in a desperate attempt to get people in the door hoping they'll come back. Or they water down their message and their service to make them more appealing. Believe it or not, raising the bar for church membership improves the retention rate. Fifty-three percent of the examples in *Comeback Churches* raised their membership requirements, usually by requiring a multi-week new members class that explained the basics of Christianity and what they as church members would be responsible for. This signaled to the visitors that as members of the congregation they were a part of something important with its own set of rights and responsibilities.

Terrace Heights Baptist Church in Yakima, Washington, saw the dramatic truth of this when they made the change. This struggling church was on the verge of closing its doors when Pastor Rob Morris shared a vision with his lay leadership to lead the congregation to a deeper spiritual level. Through committees, small groups, and Sunday sermons, Morris shared and explained his plan and at a business meeting the congregation adopted it unanimously. The new policy was that every member had to attend a new member class, then go through a yearlong "new member boot camp" of classes in spiritual foundations, spiritual formation, evangelism training, and spiritual equipping for ministry. In time the membership attrition rate dropped to almost zero.

Stetzer and Dodson added:

> If your church doesn't have a membership class process, there are many places to look for help. Find existing

> membership materials from another church in your denomination, or in your area, and adapt them to fit your church's context. Also you can look for materials and resources from Saddleback or Willow Creek or other well-known churches. . . . The pastor should lead the membership class, though other leaders can help. New people need to connect with the pastor and his vision. Invite each newcomer personally. Follow up within a week of the actual membership classes. Encourage the class attenders to review the materials and to consider the true nature of the commitment before them.
>
> Thom Rainer's research, discussed in his book *High Expectations,* reaffirms how churches with high membership requirements and expectations grow faster and are more evangelistically effective than those where membership is no big deal. "One of the key issues in closing the back door," he writes, "was the presence of a new member class as a required entry point for members. . . . Churches that *require* persons to enter membership through a new member class have a much higher retention rate than those that do not.[30]

Stetzer and Dodson added: "Most people seeking church membership do not understand the fundamentals of the Christian faith. They want to be 'good,' and church membership is a helpful part of being good. They want to be 'right,' and sense that membership is right. However, they need to be taught that none are 'good' and none are 'right.' Only by experiencing the truths of the gospel can someone truly be good and righteous."[31]

Rainer's *Breakout Churches* is a rich source of examples of churches that have survived and thrived after periods of decline.

Attitude Adjustment

Calvary Memorial Church in Oak Park, Illinois,[32] began in 1915 as a nondenominational church founded on solid biblical principles in one of the most liberal neighborhoods in the United States. Oak Park today has what may be the largest percentage of gay residents outside San Francisco. Historically Calvary Memorial has been one of only two or three churches in the community with an evangelical approach to Christianity. During the late 1980s and early 1990s, the church lost members as it struggled with several issues. One was whether or not to allow women elders, which they decided not to do. Another was whether to change to a more contemporary worship style, which they compromised on by adding a contemporary Saturday night service to the traditional Sunday one.

From 1915 to 1999, eighty-four years, Calvary Memorial grew from its founding families to a membership of about nine hundred. From 1999 to 2003, only four years, it grew from nine hundred to fifteen hundred. Their breakout event, or what Thom Rainer calls the chrysalis factor, was a change in their attitude about the community around them. They didn't change their religious beliefs; they remained the same doctrinally conservative church as always. But they made a conscious effort to reach out to their liberal neighbors. They broke out of their island of conservatism in a liberal ocean and engaged with their surroundings. In 1999 the church was almost completely white; today more than a third of the congregation is minority. There's even an active and effective counseling ministry to the homosexual community.

After the Split

First Gethsemane Baptist Church in Louisville, Kentucky,[33] survived a painful split that left only about 135 members by the time Dr. T. Vaughn Walker became pastor in 1984. Disappointed after seven years that he had made so little progress bringing in new members, Walker considered an offer to pastor another church. The new job would have meant more money, more security, and an active, growing congregation in place of a fractured and seemingly stranded church.

But Walker couldn't find any peace in the thought of leaving for what seemed to be greener pastures. After spending most of the night in prayer, he wrote the inviting church telling them he had decided to stay put at First Gethsemane. That commitment changed the course of history for that church. Dr. Walker's dedication sparked a wave of enthusiasm that spread like ripples in a pond. The church hired full-time support staff for the first time and began gradually to extend control of the budgeting process beyond the deacons and trustees. Because the change was gradual and handled with mutual respect, it was something everybody approved and benefited from. When Dr. Walker turned down his job offer in 1991, he had been pastor at First Gethsemane for seven years and attendance was running under two hundred per week. By 2003 that figure had increased to more than thirteen hundred per week. Today this vibrant congregation continues to grow and systematically updates and evaluates its ministry to keep it strong in the future.

Patient Progress

Grace Church in Middleburg Heights, Ohio,[34] is an example of how sometimes the process of turning a church around seems to take a long time, even though in God's timing it's only the blink of an eye. Donald Schaeffer founded this church in the Christian and Missionary Alliance denomination and saw attendance level off at about five hundred. Schaeffer thought that was as big a church as he could handle, and the number stayed at that level until he and some of his key lay leaders attended a Church Growth Institute seminar led by Bill Orr. The seminar message was that there's no such thing as a plateaued church; either it begins growing again, or it begins to die.

"By the time I went to that conference," Orr said, "I had gotten comfortable in ministry. Prior to that point in my ministry, there was a certain amount of self-satisfaction with the job I had done. God used that conference to create dissatisfaction. I had a drastic change in attitude toward the church's responsibility to proclaim the gospel and reach a lost world for Christ."

In the years after the seminar, the church increased lay involvement in its ministry programs, contributed more to international missions, and made many other changes, including adopting a small dwindling congregation in a nearby neighborhood.

Pastor Schaeffer founded Grace Church in 1960. It began to plateau in 1979. He went to the CGI seminar in 1985. The changes he began considering didn't start to bear fruit until 1993. But when God was ready, the church exploded. From five hundred per week in 1993 the church went to eight hundred weekly in 1998. That year Schaeffer's son Jonathan succeeded him as pastor and continued the growth. By 2003 church attendance averaged more than two thousand.

Renewal in Virginia

One of the most incredible stories I know of a shrinking church being revitalized is the history of Korean Central Presbyterian Church in Vienna, Virginia.[35] Over a quarter of a century this body of believers has had dramatic ups and downs, yet God is using it today in a mighty way, there in the shadow of our nation's capital.

When Pastor Won Sang Lee arrived in 1977, the church had just weathered a split that left it with only about thirty attending. In only two years Lee saw the church grow more than 400 percent to 130 people. Then a rift developed between Pastor Lee and some of the elders over minor issues like whether or not the congregation should be allowed to clap while singing hymns. After two years of friction, the dissident elders left and took about a third of the members with them. However the elders who were left encouraged Lee in his ministry and agreed to pray for him every day.

With the dissident group out of the picture, Korean Central Presbyterian began a steady and unbroken climb in membership. A year after the second split, membership had doubled. Today this congregation that bottomed out at thirty people numbers more than four thousand and shows no signs of slowing down.

Crisis at Xenos

The story of Xenos Christian Fellowship in Columbus, Ohio,[36] is proof that a better church isn't always a bigger church and also that effective Christian worship can sometimes take unorthodox forms. Xenos began in 1970 as an informal group of Ohio State students holding Bible studies in a boardinghouse basement. They met for twelve years before forming a formal organization and hiring their first paid staff. Their name comes from the Greek word for a sojourner in a foreign land. By 1991 more than thirty-eight hundred people attended a Xenos service every week. That was also the year when problems originated for the group's resistance to organizational hierarchy and anything smacking of "establishment." There was no real accountability among the leaders, which was fine when it was a college Bible study but unworkable as a large fellowship of believers.

The founders had no real experience. Counseling ministries had gotten caught up in pop psychology and drifted far away from biblical standards. Some of the attenders embraced the charismatic movement. When responsible leaders tried to confront some of these issues, many people in the group, used to a "do your own thing" approach, resisted being told what to do. The resulting tension stretched over three years; during that time fourteen hundred people left the church.

As the dust cleared, elders asked the pastor, Dennis McCallum, to write a vision paper for the church. A servant team infused the church with new levels of structure and accountability. Lay leaders were required to meet the character qualifications of 1 Timothy 3: "Above reproach, the husband of one wife, self-controlled, sensible, respectable, hospitable, an able teacher, not addicted to wine, not a bully but gentle, not quarrelsome, not greedy—one who manages his own household competently, having his children under control with all dignity. . . . Furthermore, he must have a good reputation among outsiders, so that he does not fall into disgrace and the Devil's trap" (vv. 2–4, 7).

Xenos Christian Fellowship emerged from their crisis stronger than ever. Today it is a thriving evangelical church with an attendance of 4,200 and 160 full-time and part-time employees. Its leaders acknowledge the pain they went through but the necessity of the crisis. They got stronger by getting smaller, then went on to new heights. Their evangelistic ministry today, especially in the inner city, is second to none. Clearly they're not a traditional church with traditional problems. But their story reinforces the truth that you can't build your church with a standard checklist. You have to pray diligently, see where God is heading, and move your church boldly in that direction.

The Saddleback Phenomenon

Though not strictly a shrinking church that changed direction, Saddleback Church in Orange County, California, outside Los Angeles, is a textbook example of a growing church.[37] Its pastor, Rick Warren, admits he took an unorthodox approach to building his congregation and repeats a warning I've already given: don't copy another church's successful growth or turn-around plan unless you have the same problems and opportunities. The point of this and other examples is to show not that one solution works all the time but that each church needs patiently to chart its own course of action.

In 1973 while he was still in college, Rick heard W. A. Criswell, legendary pastor of First Baptist Church in Dallas, speak and felt God calling him as a pastor. Shaking hands with the famous preacher afterward, Rick was surprised when Criswell said he felt specially called to pray for him and did so on the spot. The next year Rick was a student missionary in Japan when he ran across an old magazine article about Donald McGavran, whom we've met already as the father of the church growth movement. That day, Warren later wrote, "I felt God directing me to invest the rest of my life discovering the principles—biblical, cultural, and leadership principles—that produce healthy, growing churches."

In 1979 as Rick was finishing his seminary studies, he discovered that the three most unchurched states in America were Washington, Oregon, and California, and that the fastest growing area of the entire nation was in Orange County, California's Saddleback Valley. At the end of the year, Rick, his young wife, Kay, and their four-month-old baby arrived in the valley with a U-Haul truck full of their modest possessions, rented a condominium, and began gathering prayer and financial support for a new church.

Rick spent weeks walking through the neighborhood listening to what people wanted in a church and what they didn't like about church. He visited other churches and talked with pastors throughout the community. He and a group that had started a Bible study in his home hand-addressed fifteen thousand letters to neighbors inviting them to the first official worship service, scheduled for Easter Sunday, April 6, 1980. That morning 205 people joined Rick and his small group in the theater of Laguna Hills High School. Most of the congregation were "unchurched Southern Californians. We had hit our target right in the bull's-eye," he wrote.

As attendance grew, Saddleback used seventy-nine different worship locations during the first fifteen years. After that they built a twenty-three-hundred-seat tent with running water and air conditioning and held four services per weekend. Finally, when their attendance reached ten thousand per weekend, they built their first permanent building.

As Rick sums it up, "A great commitment to the Great Commandment and the Great Commission will grow a great church." Then he shares the purpose of the purpose-driven church: "To bring people to Jesus and membership in his family, develop them to Christlike maturity, and equip them for their ministry in the church and life mission in the world, in order to magnify God's name."

Churches on the upswing have a realistic view of their programs and the effect of their community outreach. Your church is where it is to serve the people of God who live and work around you. Get to know them. Reach out and invite them to know your church and your Lord. Congregations get better and stronger when they extend the hand of Christian fellowship to their neighbors. This attitude contributes to growth, and it's also the product of growth. Commitment to meeting people where they live, both literally and figuratively, is a sure sign that a church is headed in the right direction.

Heading toward Evangelism

When an organization repeats the same action time and again, you can be sure it's going to produce the same results. This seems like an incredibly simple thought, yet we've all seen churches heading down the tubes while plaintively shouting, "What's the matter? Why can't we break out of this slump?" They can't recover because they keep doing the same things that got them in a fix in the first place. Churches that are failing to thrive have to do things differently, or else they'll keep right on failing. Even though they may be busy doing many good things, they are not engaged in the essentials of growth. You might say they're driving to all sorts of important and beneficial places, but they're never putting gas in the tank or performing engine maintenance. Because its drive mechanism is ignored, a church like that won't keep running for long.

Churches that stop shrinking and start growing are likely to have a change of heart in how they engage the community around them. They don't lope blindly along doing whatever comes to mind, never planning but just grasping at straws and hoping for the best. They carefully consider their goals as a Christian fellowship, look at what they're doing to reach those goals, and study how they can do it better. Leaders in these churches gather information about the community and what it lacks. They look at the mosaic of churches in the area and see what pieces of the picture are missing. They move ahead with an awareness of what the neighborhood needs and what they can do to meet those needs.

Nurturing New Shoots

Rick Warren showed us an extreme example of this as he planned his Saddleback Church. Before scheduling the first service, he talked to pastors and polled residents all over the community to see what they didn't like about organized religion, what they needed spiritually, and what would make them comfortable. He spent time learning what didn't work. Not many church leaders will go to that much trouble; consequently not many have ever seen the historic level of growth his research eventually produced.

Shrinking churches generally don't go out of their way to reach into the community. They circle the wagons and hunker down. This response only accelerates the pace of their decline. Growing churches look outward, continually reviewing their structures and programs in light of opportunities on the horizon. Breakout churches tend to have better functioning Sunday schools and other internal organizations than churches remaining on the plateau. From this strong and steady base, they can reach out to the neighborhood to build their membership and influence, then further expand their reach. Churches that intentionally add new units are those that grow. Don't wait for growth to plant a new church because you might wait forever. Nurture a new worship community by funding a church plant or financially supporting a sister congregation. It increases your sphere of Christian influence even as it helps other congregations. Growth becomes an accepted and expected component of your church operations, and that's a benefit for churches everywhere. The pastor of a breakout church is going to spend far more time equipping, sending out, and supporting new worship units than those who have a nongrowth attitude.

When I took over my current pastorate at Taylors First Baptist, I told the congregation we would be entering the most expensive building program in the history of the church. It would involve a new look at all our organizations and structures. While most people were enthusiastically in favor of change because they saw in a general sense what was happening to the church and wanted the ongoing growth and development to continue, they were willing to change everything except what they liked. A church must take an honest look at whether its structures are working and be appropriately aggressive in reining in the ones that no longer serve a useful purpose.

Can a church in transition be involved in evangelistic outreach and visitation? What if the program is in a poor or blighted area? With God's help the seeds planted in an outreach program will grow, but that's up to God. The act of planting, though, highlights one of the greatest contrasts between breakout churches and plateaued ones. Obviously a visitation or outreach program will not in and of itself bring growth. The program must be linked to and a natural result of a growth attitude that permeates the congregation.

Breakout churches are much more likely than others to have weekly visitation programs that capture the enthusiasm and heart of people and give them a way to put their energy and willingness to serve into action. People out there in the world don't know you care about them unless you show them you do. We live in a time when, ironically, we have more ways than ever to connect with one another but have never been more lonely. With e-mail, the Internet, BlackBerry phones, and all the rest, we are intensely plugged into the world if we want to be. But that leaves less time for genuine, meaningful personal communication. We get out of the habit of knocking on a neighbor's door or calling a friend just to say hello and not for any particular reason. Meeting the community in the flesh is a key component of a healthy church.

L.E.A.D.

At Taylors First Baptist Church we are still in the process of developing a growth attitude. We're nowhere near where we need to be in this area. However, we have launched a new program to improve our outreach that involves lots of people in our congregation and is truly helping to keep the energy level up and our community connection stronger. It's called the L.E.A.D. team process.

L.E.A.D. involves a large number of *locators* whose role is to find and contact prospects for our church. There are several ways to do this, but experience has taught us that, in our community at least, the Welcome Wagon mailing list is the best source of new arrivals. We send letters to all newcomers who are within reasonable driving distance of our church, then follow up later with a phone call. The locators also sometimes simply go door-to-door in neighborhoods around our church.

Second are the team members involved in *evangelization*. Once the locators have done their work, they hand off their lists to others who take on the critical task of presenting the gospel message. These days it takes a special kind of person and a servant's willing heart to walk up to a stranger's door and ask for an opportunity to share the good news. Plenty of tools are available to help them tackle this task. One is the FAITH Sunday school evangelism training process developed by LifeWay Christian Resources. Another is the NET program from the North American Mission Board of the Southern Baptist Convention, which equips Christians in today's post-Christian culture to share their testimony in a culturally relevant way.

We have chosen to develop our own program using a gospel tract, "You Matter," written especially for us. It's sent from my office, and it begins by telling readers that they matter to the Lord, to our church, and to me. I share with them what is arguably the most important verse in the Bible for spiritual seekers, John 3:16: "For God loved the world in this way: He gave His One and Only Son, so that everyone who believes in Him will not perish but have eternal life."

I invite them to church, assure them God has purpose for their lives, and share the good news that God forgives them of their human sins and offers eternal life through Jesus Christ.

I also offer them a "time back guarantee." "If you feel that your time [in church] is wasted," I say, "let me know, and I will repay you in time by washing your car, cutting your grass, or whatever you would like. You do not get that kind of guarantee in many places, do you?" It's a simple offer, but it gets people's attention before they can say, "Oh, more junk mail," and toss it in the trash.

Whatever method you use, you must place strong emphasis on the people going out into the community. It's no secret that, especially in urban settings, people generally are skittish and often offended by the presence of church visitors. However, in most places across our nation, people are still receptive to a caring, loving, sensitive visit from concerned persons. L.E.A.D. members expect initial resistance. They don't press hard or do any fast talking. After all, they're not selling vacuum cleaners, so they shouldn't act like they are. They are there to share a treasury of life-changing, life-giving information, and knowing that gives them strength and confidence to get through any initial skepticism on the part of the other person. Team members learn to be good listeners and to explain the message from the prospect's point of view. They're not overbearing or insistent. They know all they can do is present the gospel and pray that they will open their hearts to His love and His message of salvation.

A third team *assists* in the L.E.A.D. process. These volunteers help with nursery care, pray for those going on neighborhood visits, take care of information packets for visitors who have come in response to outreach efforts, and so forth. While not on the front lines, this group is a strong and essential link in the evangelism chain. They remind me of some of the missionaries who work for Wycliffe Bible Translators. This organization is dedicated to translating the Bible into every language, including some with only a handful of speakers and many languages without any written form at all. So before they can translate, they have to invent an alphabet and written grammar for the language! In order to do that, translators are supported in the field by people who don't translate but who make it possible for others to do so: teachers for the translators' children, doctors, administrators, and other support staff.

We also have a group involved in the fourth L.E.A.D. category, *discipleship*. These are the ones who disciple new believers the program has attracted. They also encourage discipleship within Sunday school classes. The team uses a mentoring process that matches up new families with families of established church members. Once a family makes it through the front door, we want to do all we can to see that they feel welcome, understood, and spiritually fulfilled.

It is important for the church to see its pastor as a leader in evangelistic outreach and visitation. They need to know that he is leading people to Christ and equipping the church to do so. Like many pastors, I personally call every first-time visitor early in the week after they come to worship with us. After all, that's our job description according to Ephesians 4:12: "The training of the saints in the work of ministry, to build up the body of Christ."

Everybody Can Evangelize

L.E.A.D. teams are the high-profile vanguards of our evangelism process, but evangelism is every Christian's business. *Comeback Churches* identifies three ways the Bible tells us that everyone in the church body can help.

First, everybody can pray for the various teams of locators, evangelizers, assisters, and disciplers. They can pray for specific team members, specific events, or the program in general. In 1 Timothy 2:1–4 Paul wrote, "I urge that petitions, prayers, intercessions, and thanksgivings to be made for everyone, for kings and all those who are in authority, so that we may lead a tranquil and quiet life in all godliness and dignity. This is good, and it pleases God our Savior, who wants everyone to be saved and to come to the knowledge of the truth."

Next, everybody can bring a guest to church. You don't have to be on any team to extend an invitation. In fact, asking someone you know to come to church is probably more likely to succeed than asking a stranger. As John 1:40–42 reads, "Andrew, Simon Peter's brother, was one of the two who heard John and followed [Christ]. He first found his own brother Simon and told him, 'We have found the Messiah' (which means 'Anointed One'), and he brought Simon to Jesus."

Third, everybody can spread the Word, telling friends, neighbors, and others about Christ when the opportunity presents itself, just like Paul recommended his young friend Timothy should do in 2 Timothy 4:5: "Keep a clear head about everything, endure hardship, do the work of an evangelist, fulfill your ministry."

It's a simple and straightforward process, and it fits our cultural longing for personal outreach and simplicity in an ever more impersonal and complicated culture. All these suggestions, from following the Welcome Wagon to chatting with your friends, are easy, simple steps. I think Thom Rainer has it right in his book with Eric Geiger titled *Simple Church,* where he observes:

> Simple is in.
>
> Complexity is out. Out of style at least.
>
> Ironically people are hungry for simple because the world has become much more complex. The amount of information accessible to us is continually increasing. The ability to interact with the entire world is now possible. Technology is consistently advancing at a rapid pace.
>
> The result is a complicated world with complex and busy lives. And, in the midst of complexity, people want to find simplicity. They long for it, seek it, pay for it, even dream of it. Simple is in. Simple works. People respond to simple.
>
> The simple revolution has begun.[38]

He continues, "Churches with a simple process for reaching and maturing people are expanding the kingdom. Church leaders who have designed a simple biblical process to make disciples are effectively advancing the movement of the gospel. Simple churches are making a big impact.

"Conversely, complex churches are struggling and anemic [and shrinking!]. Churches without a process or with a complicated process for making disciples are floundering."[39]

I also share Rainer's point that this has nothing to do with doctrine or conviction or theology. None of that is changed.

Sharing from the Heart

Greg Laurie shares some insightful observations on witnessing in his book *The Upside Down Church*. He made all kinds of mistakes when he first tried reaching out to others, "a bona fide member of the Soul Patrol, out prowling for unbelievers to convert." He cites a survey in *Christianity Today* magazine listing the three reasons Christians most often gave for not wanting to witness: (1) They're not "professional" and can't do it as effectively as a pastor or someone specially trained; (2) they're too timid; and (3) they're afraid of how people will react.[40]

Both the Christian doing the witnessing and the non-Christian doing the listening are uncomfortable about the whole process. Many Christians are timid in part because they were once those non-Christians who insisted, "Get out of my face!" whenever someone approached them with a gospel message. Plenty of people, including some pastors, are skittish or even petrified at the thought of speaking about the gospel. Laurie writes that "the true gospel message is inherently confrontational."

Because people are nervous to start with, they make more of a hash of things than if they approached the subject in a more offhand way. They come off as pushy or tactless or both. Unfortunately there are a lot of Christians who don't seem to have a lot of tact. Laurie continues, "When the Bible says preach, it doesn't necessarily mean you have to yell or be rude. Some perfectly friendly people turn into 'droids' or tape recordings when they start to talk about Jesus." Be conversational, be sincere, avoid biblical jargon non-Christians won't understand, and speak from your heart.

It will encourage you to know that the people you approach to share the Bible with probably aren't as smug and secure as they might seem on the surface. Like all of us, they walk around with their game faces on, ready to do their daily battle with the world. They have no intention of revealing their needs or fears to you. I agree with Laurie that everybody out there on the sidewalk has invisible needs that only Christ can satisfy.

They're spiritually empty, walking around with an emptiness that only Christ can fill.

They're lonely, even if they're outwardly busy and popular. Human beings long for close, steadfast, unconditional relationships that are extremely rare. Except that Christ can bring that relationship from Himself into every human heart. Furthermore, Laurie says, only Christ actually comes and dwells within us and makes his home in us.

People are guilty and feel their guilt. You may have heard the admonition from Romans many times that "all have sinned and fall short of the glory of God" (3:23). They will be so relieved and so comforted to know that God forgives them and makes it possible for them to forgive themselves.

People are afraid to die. Without a sure knowledge of God, death is a horrible end to think about. The only peace comes from knowing that Christ in heaven has prepared a place for us and is waiting with open arms to welcome all who believe in Him.

Empty, lonely, guilty, afraid to die. These people need Jesus. Christians who are reaching out to them must remember the longings only Jesus can satisfy. Thinking about that, as you approach someone to share your faith with them, should help you remember that, despite those butterflies in your stomach, you've got information that they need, that deep down they want, that can transform their life and their eternity.

Evangelism Defined

In *Ripe for Harvest,* Lewis A. Drummond raises the question of exactly what we're doing when we become evangelicals for the faith.[41] Evangelism isn't preaching, proselytizing, or persuading someone to make a decision for Christ. It is plainly proclaiming the Word of God. Drummond has collected other definitions:

> To evangelize is so to present Christ Jesus in the power of the Holy Spirit that men shall come to put their trust in God through Him, to accept Him as their Savior, and serve Him as their King in the fellowship of His church.
>
> —Archbishop of Canterbury Committee on Evangelism

> Evangelism is going to the people outside. It is the proclamation of the good news of God in Jesus Christ to "Them that are without." It is the sheer work of the herald. . . . He blows the trumpet and demands to be heard.
>
> —W. E. Sangster, Methodist pastor, London

> Evangelism is the task of reaching outside the church to bring people to faith in Christ and membership in His church.
>
> —George Sweazy, professor, Princeton Seminary

> Evangelism is one beggar telling another beggar where to find bread.
>
> —D. T. Niles, missiologist, Sri Lanka

> Evangelism is a concerted, self-conscious effort to confront the unbeliever with the truth about and the claims of Christ with a view to challenging and leading that unbeliever into repentance toward God and faith in our Lord Jesus Christ and thus into the fellowship of His church that spiritual growth may occur.
>
> —Lewis A. Drummond

Evangelism is an essential component of Southern Baptist Convention churches, a part of the statement of faith that ties us together. I should say here that we're a denomination that generally rejects creeds and compulsory actions of all sorts. The Southern Baptist Convention is a voluntary, advisory organization that lifts up the priesthood of the believer: each Christian has a personal, individual relationship with God that requires no clergyman or church bureaucracy to be complete. However, in 1925 *The Baptist Faith and Message* was published to declare those distinctives that clearly delineate our denominational position on bedrock Christian issues. It has been revised since then, most recently in 2000. Here's what that statement says about a church's need to reach out with evangelism:

> It is the duty and privilege of every follower of Christ and of every church of the Lord Jesus Christ to endeavor to make disciples of all nations. The new birth of man's spirit by God's Holy Spirit means the birth of love for others. Missionary effort on the part of all rests thus upon a spiritual necessity of the regenerate life, and is expressly and repeatedly commanded in the teachings of Christ. The Lord Jesus Christ has commanded the preaching of the gospel to all nations. It is the duty of every child of God to seek constantly to win the lost to Christ by verbal witness undergirded by a Christian lifestyle, and by other methods in harmony with the gospel of Christ.

The final word on the matter comes, of course, from Christ Himself: "This is what is written: the Messiah would suffer and rise from the dead the third day, and repentance of sins would be proclaimed in His name to all the nations, beginning at Jerusalem. You are witnesses of these things" (Luke 24:46–48).

For most people the first thing we think of when we hear the word *evangelism* is the task of spreading the gospel using the Bible. Yes, that's the ultimate goal. But evangelism today has far more faces and facets than that. There are many, many ways to reach out to others on behalf of Jesus by helping, serving, and loving our neighbors. In the short term, witnessing for Christ may have nothing obvious to do with Scripture and everything to do with an oil change.

Taking It to the Streets

Growing churches have to develop and nurture people-centered ministries that are outwardly focused. You can't just keep preaching to the same crowd every week and stay huddled in your comfort zone. You've got to take the message to the streets. When I came to Taylors, they had a ministry to members that was second to none, but they had no concept of how to reach the lost and hurting in our community. The result was that we had the reputation in the neighborhood as a rich, white, snobby church.

Our shortcomings as a church affect us, but they also affect the community at large in ways we can scarcely imagine. In our case we unintentionally made Christians seem cold, distant, and self-absorbed to the potential church members around us. Without meaning to, we came off as people who acted like we were better than everybody else. This misunderstanding about who we were had been going on for a generation or more. The church leaders and I made a conscious effort to change the perception outsiders had of us. It took time, resources, patience, and a few ruffled feathers. But now our neighbors at every level of society know we care about them. The new outreach programs we put in place have had both immediate and long-term impact.

Churches with a passion for service and a growth-oriented attitude are more likely to conduct specialized ministries and to have an increased emphasis of ministry to the community. Instead of exclusively taking care of their own, those churches also believe that they are to reach out and help persons in time of need. Some churches have done this in an extremely effective way.

When I got to town, Taylors was one of the most inwardly focused churches I had ever seen. Its ministry to its own members was intricate and organized. One of the greatest organizations ever imagined was in place to make sure that sick and hurting people were cared for. However, the church didn't know how to carry that passion out into the world around us.

Serving Our Neighbors

We came up with a range of servant evangelism projects that have been responsible for changing the community's perception about us. Some of these projects are decidedly out of the ordinary. Several address practical needs that have no apparent connection with spiritual matters. For example, our congregation and our community have a lot of single mothers. These brave women have a rough time juggling work, school, child care, meals, housework, and everything else they have to do. The last thing on earth most of them are thinking about is keeping their cars in good running order. Yet because they're so busy, and probably living on a tight budget, an automotive breakdown can be a disaster.

There are men in our church who know lots about cars and enjoy working on them. So we came up with the idea of a quarterly oil change service for single moms. This has become an extremely effective outreach as well as a way for us to break down negative stereotypes. More than one hundred single mothers come to take advantage of this service. While the men of our church are working on their cars, the women of our church are witnessing, feeding, and ministering to these women and their families. This time of interaction gives us the chance to make other services available too. During a recent oil change day, our church distributed new school supplies that had been donated for the purpose.

Sunday school classes have become involved in a huge array of servant evangelism projects. Every age and ministry group in the church now sees outreach as a crucial part of their work. Certain days are set aside as servant evangelism days to introduce ourselves to the community and make them feel welcome. This will have long-term impact on the health of our church and the reach of the gospel into our neighborhood.

Growing churches and large churches are often accused of caring only about numbers and nothing about quality. While this may be true in isolated cases, I do not believe it is true in more than a handful of them. I don't think most large churches get large by doing things wrong. In most instances there is a serious emphasis on spiritual renewal and deep, abiding prayer ministries. In churches that have broken out of declining/plateaued status, there is serious emphasis on prayer ministries.

At Taylors First Baptist Church, we have a multitude of prayer ministries, including a twenty-four-hour-per-day prayer room on site. We also have a variety of other ministries that are pulled together in a ministry called God's 3000. Our goal is to involve three thousand persons in some kind of ongoing intercessory prayer ministry. We are approaching the 2,000 mark as of this writing. We are asking children, students, and young, median, and senior adults to gather in various prayer ministries. It has made a tremendous impact on our church! We see people praying in several specific areas: some are waging general spiritual warfare; others lift up earnest, ongoing prayer for pastors, staff, ministries, and committees; still others volunteer for more general prayer needs. E-mail is used to send out constant reminders and updates for prayer assignments. God's 3000 is truly the foundation of the success of our church.

Prayer is at the core of church growth, but there's nothing wrong with taking care of practical needs of the people and fulfilling a natural desire for fellowship. Jesus preached the gospel tirelessly, but He also fed the masses with loaves and fishes, provided wine for a wedding feast, and otherwise ministered to the physical and emotional needs of His listeners and followers. People who don't go to church often have strange misconceptions about Christian faith and practice. Once you bring them in with, say, an offer for an oil change, they realize Christians are a lot more friendly and more approachable than they thought. Their presence (then or at a later time) creates an opportunity to steer the discussion toward matters of faith.

At Taylors First Baptist we've put a strong emphasis on outreach. The results have been a blessing in many ways. First, it has involved many church members in real-world evangelism for the first time. Second, for Christians with a heart for service who don't feel equipped to evangelize by presenting a Bible message, these opportunities let them serve the cause of Christ doing something they feel confident in. Third, many grateful people know us—and know our Savior—who wouldn't have given our church a second glance in the past.

Impact Greenville

As an umbrella identity to help organize and track our outreach ministry, we launched Impact Greenville. This is a full-court press into the Greenville community to serve others in the name of Christ. In the past year more than four thousand people, ages ten to eighty-nine, pitched in to assist with twenty-five different ministries or agencies. Six groups hosted neighborhood or community service projects to build relationships. Forty-five classes or ministry groups worked alongside one another and gave of their time. Labors of love included yard work, cleaning, block parties, cookouts, car washes, clerical work, replacing blinds, bottled water distribution, sorting clothes, painting, and cookie deliveries.

Impact Greenville has been a tremendous success in making others aware of our church and our commitment to Christian service. A few sample comments from the people who served will give you an idea of how dramatically this program built the reputation of our congregation and gave our members a chance to extend the hand of Christian fellowship, one encounter and one heart at a time:

> People just could not believe that we would do this [neighborhood block party] for free. . . . We had people offer us money. They were so appreciative.
>
> We all felt very blessed to make a difference and brighten the lives of the Carriage House residents. [Carriage House is a residential psychological treatment center.] This team's efforts saved them over $2,500.
>
> What a joy to share our love for Jesus and for the firemen and policemen of our community.
>
> The haircuts provided by one of our team members made the residents of the Miracle Hill Boys Home feel so special as someone gave them individual attention.
>
> I needed sixteen people for the job and God came with forty!
>
> People are much more receptive to the gospel if they know you love them. The building of this relationship is the heartbeat of Impact Greenville.

I don't mean to brag about what our church has done. Everything is on account of God's grace and is for His glory, not ours. But I know the inner workings of my own church better than any other, and if I'm going to go into detail about church outreach, I may as well use the examples I'm most familiar with. And there's more.

Many Hands, Many Hearts

Angel Food Ministries is a nonprofit organization that provides financial support and healthful groceries to more than 500,000 families across the country, including families at Taylors. Each month they offer a box of assorted family food items for $25 that would be worth at least $50 in the grocery store, giving families a variety of healthful food at substantial discounts. When participants come to pick up their order at church once a month, it provides a wonderful time of fellowship. It gives nonmembers another reason to be interested in our church. And it gives those who wish an opportunity to donate food to those in need.

Piedmont Women's Center training prepares volunteers to help women with crisis pregnancies find medical help, compassionate understanding, Christian counseling and prayer support, and a home for their child if they so desire.

By His Hands is a new outreach ministry that delivers meals on Wednesday nights to shut-ins and those of our neighbors who need a helping hand. This is an example of the kind of outreach that doesn't take evangelism training and doesn't require volunteers to witness in the usual way. A warm, delicious meal delivered free is a pretty good conversation starter, particularly when it comes with a cordial visit and a few minutes of discussion. Once inside, the volunteer may take advantage of opportunities to pray for the person and help them out with other needs.

The Kensington Apartments ministry is a weekly Bible study for men in this apartment building. We have a core group of men who are faithful in attending and eager to listen and participate in discussions. Praise the Lord for men who are willing to share and learn from one another as they discover God's purpose for their lives.

Our *Women's Scrapbooking/Crop Night* is a monthly get-together for those who enjoy this hobby. This event is a fun evening of fellowship for women. We praise the Lord for relationships that have formed from this group.

In South Carolina we have a large and growing Spanish-speaking immigrant population. These residents tend to be low income, wary of any sort of authority, and unfamiliar with Protestant Christianity. Language and cultural barriers isolate them from the community at large. It would be easy to overlook this population. Instead, we've made it a priority to expand the church's relationship with them. We've planted *Iglesia Bautista Betania,* a Baptist church with services in Spanish. Children there are welcome to participate in Taylors First Baptist Sunday school activities.

Church plants are a proven way for a church to expand its reach in a region. With few exceptions people aren't going to drive all the way across town to go to your church. The solution is to take your church to them. We have a tradition of planting new churches, helping a satellite congregation get going, supporting it financially, and providing leadership until it becomes self-supporting. Our goal is to establish one plant each year as the Lord leads.

Recently we assisted in starting *BridgePointe Church,* a church plant for the unchurched. The first service there was in the spring of 2006, and by September the congregation was meeting regularly every week. It's too soon to say whether this new effort will attract enough worshippers to sustain it in the long run, but so far the results are encouraging. We're working hard and praying hard that BridgePointe will succeed in the name of Christ.

Training and Follow-up

Part of Impact Greenville is making sure the church volunteers who participate have the tools and training they need for the job and for follow-up after the projects, as necessary. In some cases we had existing mission groups that could step in to fill a need. The program notifies and equips Sunday school leaders for monthly service opportunities, which makes use of the preexisting Sunday school structure. The Impact Greenville team, along with all the rest of the church, has set up a prayer network for all the programs and the neighbors they reach.

Impact Greenville has decision counselors trained and ready for ministry opportunities and to be available for ministry visits after projects are completed. It has a trained team to be available for the single mom's oil change, Taylors free medical clinic, and other outreach-based opportunities.

Impact Greenville also partners with ongoing community organizations with compatible goals, meeting the needs of the people while furthering the kingdom through evangelism and discipleship. Another part of the program is making sure we get the word out. In years past we might have had to do that with bulletin flyers or pulpit announcements. In the cyber-age we have a lot more choices. We use our church Web site and other media to keep the church aware of what God is doing in the lives of His people as a testimony to others.

By expanding the scope of local ministry, we can more greatly influence the community for Christ. Consider all that can be done together to reach out to Greenville in the year ahead. As people are better equipped and awareness is increased, we anticipate that God will accomplish even greater things through us in the future.

Taking It around the World

We also look for ways to expand our reach through ministries outside our city. After Katrina and the other disastrous hurricanes of the summer of 2005, South Carolina Baptist volunteers were mobilized to assist victims of natural and man-made destruction. The multifaceted disaster relief ministry in South Carolina is a ministry of the North American Mission Board, which acts as a sending agency for state units. In other words, assignments for disaster relief units are given to the state Baptist conventions through the North American Mission Board. This is a good example of using existing ministries and administrative structures to support a new ministry in order to meet a new kind of need. These volunteers allow others to see Jesus in them through loving response to their needs. Training is required to go on a deployment with any disaster relief team. Two training sessions are offered each year by the South Carolina Baptist Convention.

Looking even farther afield, our church is ramping up its involvement in out-of-state and foreign missions. While there will always be mission opportunities close to home, working in a distant field of service gives our members new enthusiasm for service and a new appreciation for how much the world needs Jesus' message of salvation and redemption. The resources spent on these trips are invaluable for the dedication they stir up in those who participate. To some it is a life-changing experience.

Depending on the destination, the groups range in size from about six to sixteen. They are specially trained for work in that area, learning as much of the culture and tradition as possible, plus a few words of the local language. These teams take the gospel literally to the ends of the earth.

In North Waterboro, Maine, we helped build a new church for a young body of believers in partnership with the Maine Baptist Association. Our team assisted in a variety of construction jobs coupled with the opportunity to impact the local community through servant evangelism. Details of our work were defined by the construction skills of the people who signed up to go.

Moving still farther away from familiar surroundings, we sent an evangelism team to Calgary, Canada, in the summer of 2006 with the hopes of planting a new church in South Calgary. The group hosted block parties in targeted neighborhoods, along with sports camps and other activities to connect with the families there. Our church has developed strong ties with the Canadian Baptists as a result, and we will continue our annual trips there, praying that God will do great things as we serve Him there.

We also sponsored a team headed in the other direction, to Mexico to help with church planting, evangelism, and construction.

Following the lead of our denomination's International Mission Board, we will continue to come alongside the great work of evangelizing this area of Mexico in desperate need of the Savior.

Africa has seen generations of dedicated missionaries and evangelists reach out to its often isolated and primitive cultures. A team of volunteers from our church traveled to the bush country of Zambia, the central African nation formerly known as Rhodesia, where the native population has never heard the name of Jesus. Our team worked alongside pastors to help share the good news of Christ, going hut to hut with them, taking the salvation message to someone who probably has never even seen a European before. Participants lived in the rustic conditions of the bush, getting a brief taste of an exotic lifestyle that most of us can't even imagine. The team also helped to encourage and equip church leaders in their work there.

For the ultimate in extreme evangelism, how about witnessing in the Himalayas? A team from Taylors First Baptist journeyed to the remotest part of the world to intercede for the lost there. Again partnering with the International Mission Board, these volunteers had the honor and responsibility of talking with and praying for people very different from us, and yet the same: all of us are in need of the Savior. This team will walk the settlements there, praying for the millions who do not know our Jesus as Lord.

From local outreach through Impact Greenville to the jungles of Africa and the top of the world in the Himalayas, Taylors First Baptist is taking the name of Jesus far and wide. We started small with ministries in our neighborhood, then extended our programs to the region, to other areas of the United States, then Canada and Mexico, and then around the world. Our idea and commitment have remained consistent from the beginning. We felt God calling us to focus our attention outward to address the needs of a fallen world. We have looked outward and tried to fill the spiritual void we saw there. God rewarded our efforts by giving us the means to reach out to those areas. We began by changing oil for single mothers down the street; now we're sending messengers of Christ to the four corners of His earth.

Growth wasn't our primary motivation in taking the gospel to the streets. Our aim above all else was to serve Christ and be obedient to His will. But in our case, as in the case of so many other healthy and growing churches, that attitude of service to others gave us a spiritual strength and a dynamism visitors found attractive because they saw God at work through these programs. They in turn brought us their own skills and enthusiasm, which enabled our outreach efforts to grow larger, which reached more skilled and enthusiastic people who became members. And so we reached the critical stage where our growth was self-sustaining.

At the same time our evangelism work has thrived, we've kept close watch on our Sunday worship services. Many people, especially visitors and recent members, know us only by what they experience at Sunday church. While all these other areas of worship and outreach are important, Sunday worship is the most prominent and visible part of our community of faith. So we have to make sure it shines as brightly as we can make it.

Putting Out the Welcome Mat

We've drifted a long way at this point in the story from my South Carolina stomping grounds to talk about the importance of evangelism in reviving a shrinking church. But as you look outward to serve your neighborhood and the greater community, you can't ignore the worship experience right at home. What happens in your church on Sunday morning is the only thing most potential members know about you. It defines who will feel comfortable and welcome at your service and who won't. A growing church has a service that reverently upholds the gospel and at the same time meets the people at their point of need.

We've already seen how the issue of worship style, especially regarding music, can be a divisive battle that splits church bodies into armed camps. It's a topic where emotions run high because people have passionate feelings about it. At Taylors First Baptist we have settled on a style we believe our community sees as welcoming and comfortable. There are many ways to tackle this issue, and most of them are right.

I believe there are solid boundaries around what a worship service should be: it should proclaim the gospel of Christ as given to us in the unerring Word of the Bible. It should balance the message of our sin, accountability, and judgment before God with that of

Christ's sacrifice for us: that we, though sinners, can receive the gift of eternal life when we accept Him as our personal Savior. The service should be respectful but at the same time a joyful celebration of the Holy Spirit.

Within those boundaries Christians should be encouraged to worship in whatever way they feel called to worship. Whether they're in their best suits or their most comfortable jeans is unimportant. The style of the music is far less important than its message. Considering these variables carefully and praying diligently for the Lord's guidance in matters of worship will help you and your church leadership craft a service that will strengthen your spiritual foundations and build your membership. In other words, you've got to think about what would interest your neighbors and then roll out the welcome mat.

At Taylors First Baptist Church you're welcome to come as you are. Most of our members wear casual attire on Sunday morning, though plenty of them choose traditional Sunday dress. Others are at home in denim from head to toe. The 9:00 a.m. contemporary/blended service is more casual than the 10:30 a.m. traditional service.

People who are plugged into the life of the church, beginning with Sunday attendance, will be more satisfied with their experience and more supportive of our ministries. They tend to move from passive spectators to active participants. Once they're invested in the life and work of the church, they're more likely to stay with us and more likely to recommend us to others. On our Web site and elsewhere, we make sure they know how to participate in the most popular activities here. Your church will have a different list that's best suited to your worship environment, but the idea is the same. Here's a sampling of ways for our people to participate.

Plugging In

In the digital age we're constantly looking for volunteers to help with our media ministry, and there are always people eager to get involved. This ministry is key in providing our members and guests with a rich, meaningful worship experience. Our technical team serves the Lord through audio, video, A/V reproduction, lighting, MediaShout, PowerPoint, and a variety of other media applications. The technical team also provides support for other ministries that meet on our campus throughout the week. A willing heart is all that is necessary to find a place of service in this area of ministry. We provide all the training required.

In light of the size of our congregation and the variety of musical interests and training the members have, we have eight different musical groups. But even if you have one modest choir on Sunday mornings, you can still reach out and invite participation from others who love to lift up praises in lyrics and music.

The TFBC choir exists to worship God through music and lead others to do the same. As principal leaders of the Sunday morning contemporary/blended worship service, this dedicated group joins with the sanctuary choir for special presentations throughout the year. No audition is required; only a heart for worship, a love for singing, and a commitment to weekly rehearsals and worship services are the prerequisites.

The sanctuary choir is a dynamic group of singers who serve a primary role each week in preparing hearts for the Word of God during the traditional/blended service. The sanctuary choir combines with the TFBC choir for special programs during the year. Attendance at weekly rehearsals and Sunday services and a desire to use your voice to praise God are the only requirements for participation.

"Loving God and loving each other. Making music with my friends," could be the theme song for the Legacy Singers, a gifted and experienced group of seniors. Singing in worship services several times during the year, Legacy is in much demand throughout our community for special programs and has had the opportunity to serve as the "revival choir" at numerous churches. The only requirement for Legacy Singers is a love for Christ and a love of music.

Comprised of faithful members of the TFBC music and worship ministry, Voices of Praise presents special music and adds support in the contemporary/blended service. Seeking God's face is their ultimate priority. Auditions and interview are requirements for participation in this group. The group size is limited.

A premier singing group, In His Honor has opportunities to sing during worship services and special programs throughout the year. Known for their close harmonies and a capella styling, participation is through audition only.

The sanctuary orchestra is a vital part of the music and worship ministry of Taylors First Baptist Church. Made up of musicians from all walks of life, this volunteer ensemble shares a common goal, to "praise Him with instruments! Let everything that has breath praise the Lord." The sanctuary orchestra plays each Sunday during the second service and is the core orchestra for special music and worship ministry presentations throughout the year.

The TFBC student orchestra provides a challenging opportunity for students to develop musical skills in a nonthreatening Christian environment. Several times during the year this group will share their progress during our evening worship services. A working knowledge of one's instrument is required for participation in this group for students in the sixth through twelfth grades.

The worship band is a devoted group of musicians who provide accompaniment for the Voices of Praise. The band is the core instrumental group for the Sunday contemporary/blended worship service. They also participate as members of the orchestra for special presentations during the year. Participation is through audition.

A Spirit of Celebration

This kaleidoscope of musical praise offerings pours into a worship experience that we believe honors God and welcomes all who participate. Worship is the heart and soul of a church; we want our heart and soul to be genuine, open, encouraging, and faithful to the gospel.

No matter how big a church becomes, it has to maintain a serious emphasis on spiritual renewal and deep, abiding prayer ministries. Studies show that an atmosphere of excitement in worship is directly related to spiritual renewal and prayer. Regardless of worship style, the worship experience has to be warm, sincere, vibrant, and joyful.

Time after time the Bible encourages us to worship God with a spirit of celebration. The Psalms ring with this wonderful advice. Psalm 66:2 says, "Sing the glory of His name; make His praise glorious." The first verse of Psalm 111 reads, "Hallelujah! I will praise the LORD with all my heart in the assembly of the upright and in the congregation."

If that doesn't convince you that church ought to be teeming with energy and joy, Psalm 150 is license to raise the roof:

> Hallelujah! Praise God in His sanctuary. Praise Him in His mighty heavens. Praise Him for His powerful acts; praise Him for His abundant greatness.
>
> Praise Him with trumpet blast; praise Him with harp and lyre. Praise Him with tambourine and dance; praise Him with flute and strings. Praise Him with resounding cymbals; praise Him with clashing cymbals.
>
> Let everything that breathes praise the Lord. Hallelujah!

A meaningful, Spirit-filled worship service can offset all sorts of challenges that might make people think twice about visiting your church or otherwise stunt your growth potential. Your church might be hard to get to or in an urban setting suburbanites find uncomfortable. Maybe there's not enough parking, or like at Taylors there are train tracks everywhere. People want to be a part of something that feels and smells successful.

Spruce Up the Setting

Great worship can make up for a less than great setting. Relocation is often impractical or impossible, but sprucing up the worship facilities has a powerful effect on attitude. Building programs are a major component of a growing church, but they have to be for the right reasons and can't divert emphasis or resources from the prime functions of the church. However, there are many ways in which a church can upgrade, update, and renovate so as to present an attitude of growth, caring, and quality.

Often church members have grown so accustomed to their facilities that they do not see the need to change. You may remember me mentioning that in our setting, we had Sunday school classes with the ceiling tiles literally falling down on people's heads. Nothing had been updated for more than thirty years. Now, when persons come into our facility, they see an updated, fresh, and far more modern facility. We didn't move; we chose to stay right where we were.

Let me stop a moment here to say it's important not to let the tail wag the dog when it comes to new building campaigns. One of the objections to capital campaigns is always that it diverts money from the work of the church. It's common sense to think this will happen and sometimes, unfortunately, it does. But with the right attitude and leadership it won't. And even if it does in the short term, having more room and more people in the church will generate more funds for programs and missions in the long term than the smaller group could ever have raised.

We built a multimillion-dollar new facility to replace aging and outdated buildings. I promised our people two things during the building program. First I promised that our mission giving would not decline. In fact, while we were building our new facilities, we dramatically increased our mission giving and sent out three family units to the International Mission Board in career mission service. This is the best-case scenario, using the new construction to focus on the far greater building project of adding new souls to the Christian flock.

I also promised that we would not make the building program a central core of our discussion and life. I told them that a building is nothing but a tool to do what God has called us to do. In fact,

I mentioned it so seldom that many people forgot that we were building a new facility. (It was built behind our large sanctuary and out of sight for most.) Therefore, when the dedication service came, many people were absolutely overwhelmed by this new facility. I reminded them of my promises, and we rejoiced to know that a new building had been built that had not become the definition of who we are.

Saving the *Titanic*

Churches assemble these components of worship style, facilities, and other variables in as many ways as there are churches. Every one of them has experienced lessons the rest of us can learn from. In *Comeback Churches*, pastor Scott Brooks of Wadsworth Alliance Church in Wadsworth, Ohio, recounted a story that will sound all too familiar to pastors who have taken over troubled congregations and wanted to put out a new welcome mat. He started with the fact that this body of believers had a poor opinion of itself. The members needed an attitude adjustment. They needed to feel a sense of accomplishment and success.

"The atmosphere of our church when I arrived was very similar to the *Titanic*," he said.

> People were jumping ship left and right, yet there was crew manning the pumps still convinced the ship could be saved. They were a people that had been sternly preached to and reminded about their deficiencies and what a sorry lot they were. Fellowship was almost non-existent. The church was completely empty five minutes after the service; that's how acidic the environment was. I sensed God was calling me to bring healing and encouragement. I preached through Nehemiah and compared the church to Israel [the disgraced remnant that returned from exile, which Nehemiah used to rebuild Jerusalem's walls]. . . . The church didn't need to hear

> about how messed up they were, they needed to know their pastor loved them and that God had not quit on them. Now the last person doesn't leave until 30–40 minutes after the service.

Once he helped the church recover its perspective and sense of optimism, the leadership there gave him a free hand to do whatever it took to revive their sagging prospects. The worship format underwent a transformation.

"If new Christians come in and hear a style of music they have already been listening to, their worship experience will already be familiar even though they have to learn new words. Having said that, every service we remain tied to our ancient faith through at least one hymn. We don't dare lose the rich heritage of our faith. The mandate I was given by the leadership of the church was, 'Do whatever you have to do to bring life back to our worship services.'" They agreed to a change in music style. They also replaced thirty-year-old sound equipment with new state-of-the-art gear. It was enormously expensive for them, but they were committed to making everything the best it could be. And it worked. After four years the church doubled in size.

I strongly support one warning Brooks made to his members, which is that you can't confuse sincere, thoughtful, God-inspired updating of your worship style with empty glitz and entertainment.

"Churches often rediscovered their passion for God and His mission by examining their worship. Unfortunately, some think that 'jazzing up' the worship is a quick fix. It is not. . . . In many cases, the worship of the church was once meaningful but has since lost its cultural significance."[42] We're called to worship God in spirit as well as in truth. Psalm 100:1–2 says, "Shout triumphantly to the LORD, all the earth. Serve the LORD with gladness; come before Him with joyful songs."

This is the kind of worship that expresses the joy of believers and makes a strong impact on nonbelievers. This is what Paul was thinking about when he wrote of what happens to the unbeliever's heart in a genuinely spiritual worship environment: "The secrets of his heart will be revealed, and as a result he will fall down on his face and worship God, proclaiming, 'God is really among you'" (1 Cor. 14:25).

Sampling a Style

If you do change components of your worship style to make it more contemporary and familiar, you'll be part of the historic surge in that direction that has been gaining momentum for decades. Churches may switch from traditional to contemporary or add blended elements of both styles so as not to lose the historical spiritual foundations. *Comeback Churches* reports that 90 percent of churches surveyed featured praise choruses and 71 percent of revitalized churches used guitars in their services, the same percentage as used a piano. Sixty-two percent used drums. Thirty percent used an organ. Also, 75 percent sang traditional hymns and 59 percent sang contemporary Christian music.

Yet for all the change, the authors report, "The vast majority of American churches are not contemporary."[43] They, like other church growth experts, suggest visiting growing churches in the area and seeing what they're doing. They call it an exercise in reconnaissance, "like the spies in the book of Numbers." Consider what other churches are doing and imagine how those features would go over in your own church.

Stetzer and Dodson advise in *Comeback Churches* that once you decide to go in a new direction, set up an experiment holding four different kinds of services on successive weeks: traditional (organ or piano, hymnbooks, choir robes), blended traditional (piano or electronic keyboard, praise songs, choir more relaxed), blended contemporary (maybe a drum or two and a couple of horns added to the mix), and contemporary (rockin' praise band and words on the big screen). Try them all and then have the members vote on the direction they want to go. In the authors' experience all the churches that have gone down this path have voted to change from where they were, and all have grown substantially since then.

What else do transitioning churches look at to make the welcome mat more welcoming? Fifty-three percent of recovering churches have pastors who preach verse by verse. "Being faithful to the biblical text is the key," the authors say. "Comeback churches definitely desire to be biblically faithful, but they also seek to be culturally relevant and practical."

Looking at the phenomenon of the incredible shrinking church, we've pretty much run the gamut from the big picture to the small details, looking at what pastors say, what research experts say, and of course, most important of all, what the Bible says. We determined earlier that there's no silver bullet to make a church healthy. But there *is* one tool that will equip you better than any other to pull your church out of a black hole and make it grow. It's deceptively simple (notice how that word keeps coming up), but its power is unassailable, and the results are guaranteed.

The Whole Armor of God

We looked earlier at the perspective of fear versus the perspective of faith. First Samuel 17 tells the story of Israel at war with the Philistines, a time of great trauma for the Hebrew people. You may remember the actual setting described in verse 3: "The Philistines were standing on one hill, and the Israelites were standing on another hill with a ravine between them." Then Goliath stood and said, "I defy the ranks of Israel today. Send me a man so we can fight each other!" (v. 10). The next verse follows with the real story: "When Saul and all Israel heard these words from the Philistines, they lost their courage and were terrified."

Who was the king on this occasion? Obviously the king was Saul. Was Saul willing to fight the giant? Was he willing to kill Goliath? He had a perspective of fear the same as almost everyone else.

Travel with me ahead several years to a time of another encounter between Israel and the Philistines in 1 Chronicles 20:4 and following. This time the story is different. The Israelite Sibbecai killed a Philistine named Sippai. During another battle with the Philistines, Elhanan killed Lahmi, the brother of Goliath. The next two verses tell how Jonathan, David's nephew, killed a giant who had extra fingers and toes:

> A war broke out with the Philistines at Gezer. At that time Sibbecai the Hushathite killed Sippai, a descendant of the giants, and the Philistines were subdued.
>
> Once again there was a battle with the Philistines, and Elhanan son of Jair killed Lahmi the brother of Goliath the Gittite. The shaft of his spear was like a weaver's beam.
>
> There was still another battle at Gath where there was a man of extraordinary stature with six fingers on each hand and six toes on each foot—24 in all. He, too, was descended from the giant. When he taunted Israel, Jonathan, son of David's brother Shimei, killed him. (vv. 4–7)

Wouldn't you agree that this circumstance was entirely different from the one in 1 Samuel? In the first instance everyone except one small boy is afraid to fight the giant. In the second instance, everybody seems to be in the giant-killing business. What made the difference? Why the complete about-face in perspective from fear to faith?

You'll find the key to these answers by comparing the kings in each of these situations. In the first setting the king was Saul; in the second the king was David. Which of these leaders was a giant killer *himself*? David, of course, who as a small boy had killed Goliath single-handedly with only a sling when nobody else in the whole army would face him.

When a giant-killer leads, the troops want to kill giants too.

As leaders of God's people, we need to be giant killers. We need to stop talking about it and start doing it. We need to lead by example and not by word alone. We need to be in the giant-killing business.

How do you get the fortitude to kill a giant? What can enable us, puny as we are, to pull off such a miraculous feat? The answer is faith. Too simple an answer? Let's delve a little deeper into the question and other questions that it raises: What kind of faith? Faith in what? The boy David gives them to us in his reply to Goliath's taunts in 1 Samuel 17.

Goliath said, "Come here . . . and I'll give your flesh to the birds of the sky and the wild beasts!" (v. 44).

Young David responded, "You come against me with a dagger, spear, and sword, but I come against you in the name of the LORD of Hosts, the God of Israel's armies—you have defied Him. Today, the LORD will hand you over to me. Today, I'll strike you down, cut your head off, and give the corpses of the Philistine camp to the birds of the sky and the creatures of the earth. Then all the world will know that Israel has a God, and this whole assembly will know that it is not by sword or by spear that the Lord saves, for the battle is the LORD's" (vv. 45–47).

How about that! David put his faith in the Lord God Almighty and Him alone. Saul put his faith in his battle gear and his size and strength. Saul put faith in his armor while David had faith in God's armor. Remember how Saul tried to put his armor on David thinking it would protect him? The difference is faith, and the faith that is a victorious faith is one that trusts in the right armor.

Killing the Giant

The key to killing the giant is putting on the whole armor of God. All of us today desperately need to see and follow leaders who are giant killers. However, the issue truly is perspective. If we are going to be victorious, we need to have the same perspective that David did: the perspective of faith. We cannot trust another's armor nor our own ability. We must trust the armor of God.

Paul knew this when he wrote to the church at Ephesus, producing one of the most ringing, most encouraging passages in all Scripture:

> Finally, be strengthened by the Lord and by His vast strength. Put on the full armor of God so that you can stand

> against the tactics of the Devil. For our battle is not against flesh and blood, but against the rulers, against the authorities, against the world powers of this darkness, against the spiritual forces of evil in the heavens. This is why you must take up the full armor of God, so that you may be able to resist in the evil day, and having prepared everything, to take your stand. Stand, therefore,
>
> with truth like a belt around your waist,
> righteousness like armor on your chest,
> and your feet sandaled with readiness for the gospel
> of peace.
> In every situation take the shield of faith,
> and with it you will be able to extinguish
> the flaming arrows of the evil one.
> Take the helmet of salvation,
> and the sword of the Spirit, which is God's word."
> (Eph. 6:10–17)

I want to be a giant killer. There are many out there, but God knows we need many more. I believe you want to be a giant killer too. However, let us understand that we cannot do it through education, resources, clever teaching tools, denominational resources, or ecclesiastical backing. It will be done when we learn to kill giants while wearing the armor of God, fighting God's battles.

To restore an incredible shrinking church is a formidable task because there's always a monstrous giant waiting to try to stop you! I meet regularly with pastors who have paid a high price in attempting to fight this type of giant. Some have succeeded. Some have felt it was more than they could bear. Others have been seriously wounded in the process. However I know it can be done. It's a glorious, inspiring feeling to put that monster in his place. And if I can be a giant killer, so can you.

The Bible is filled with imagery of the small and weak succeeding against overwhelming odds. Isaiah 60:22 proclaims, "The least will become a thousand, the smallest a mighty nation." The story of Jesus serving a crowd of five thousand with nothing but one small basket of loaves and fishes is the only miracle that appears in all four Gospels. It's that important. Doing great things with meager resources is a hallmark of Christian living.

A mustard seed is the prime biblical example of a tiny, seemingly insignificant part of God's creation that packs a wallop. It's one of the smallest seeds in the garden. Put an average mustard seed on a penny and it's too small to cover the date. Yet it grows into a plant more than six feet high. Matthew 13 compares the kingdom of heaven to this miniscule seed. If you have even that much faith, it can take root and thrive in the world. God is so all-powerful that even the smallest amount of His power can transform your life and your church.

Matthew 17 tells the story of a man who brought his epileptic son to Jesus' disciples hoping they could heal him, but they couldn't do it. After Jesus successfully cast out the demon that was in the boy, the boy was healed. "Why couldn't we drive it out?" the disciples asked in verse 19.

"'Because of your little faith,' He told them. 'For I assure you: If you have faith the size of a mustard seed, you will tell this mountain, "Move from here to there," and it will move. Nothing will be impossible for you'" (v. 20).

"Nothing will be impossible for you." I like the sound of that. Bringing a church back from the brink feels like moving a mountain. There are days when nothing moves at all, and many more when there's only the slightest hint of any gain. There are stubborn people to deal with, practical limitations like budgets and building sites, and no end of ways for things to go wrong. But faith the size of a mustard seed can move mountains. Power to reenergize the most lifeless of churches comes by putting on the whole armor of God.

Claiming God's power is ultimately what makes churches grow. That sounds easy, but doing it is usually a lot harder than it sounds. In their groundbreaking book *Experiencing God,* Henry Blackaby and Claude King show how we're all so impatient to get going and think that if God would just get with the program everything would be fine. The authors then explain that it isn't a matter of us bringing God into a situation where a church is on life support, pointing to the patient and saying, "Here, God, fix this!" God was there first. He has His own way of working, and it may not be—probably won't be—your way. Your task is to do all you know how to do, then wait on the Lord to work out the details and His timing and tell you what to do next.

God's greatest task is to get His people adjusted to Himself. He needs time to shape us until we are exactly what He wants us to be. Suppose you sense that God is going to do something great because of what He has said in His Word and prayer. You sense He is going to do it because of the way circumstances are working out and other believers in the church agree. Then six months pass and you still haven't seen anything great. Don't become negative and depressed and discouraged. *The God who initiates His work in a relationship with you is the One Himself who guarantees to complete it.* Watch to see what God is doing in you and in the people around you to prepare you for what He is going to do. The key is your relationship with God.[44]

When we take our cues from the world in building a church, we fall short of God's magnificent plan for us and our fellow worshippers. You can't build a church like it was a shopping center, and you can't run it like a business. Yes, it should be convenient and comfortable and attractive. Yes, it has to be organized with a sense of discipline and responsible stewardship. But a church is God's house. He will not forsake you. He will not lead you off into some dead end. He will never shrink, and neither will His church as long as we faithfully put on the armor of God every morning, scan the horizon with confidence, and head out looking for a giant before he starts looking for us.

A Parting Thought: You Can Do It!

These are times of great promise and opportunity for American churches. People everywhere are hungry for the hope, assurance, and peace of mind that only Christ can give them. Instead of being intimidated or disheartened by all the figures and trends that show church membership is declining, I hope you will look at them as signs of tremendous potential for growth.

Statistics are useful tools, but they can also make us feel like the battle is already lost and that church growth these days is a hopeless cause. Young David proved otherwise in his standoff with the giant! Don't allow yourself or your church to hide behind the excuse that "there's nothing else we can do." In spite of the general trends, there are healthy, growing churches of all sizes in every area of the country. We've seen a few of them here, and I've shared the story of congregations I have served that have grown despite all sorts of challenges. No situation is beyond the power of God; no church can get into such a deep hole that God can't get it out. It may not be on your timetable, and it may not be the way you had in mind, but you can be sure that God will use your church to His glory.

Turning around a shrinking church takes patience, faith, hard work, and a steady hand. It takes the shared vision and cooperation of all the church leaders and membership. And it takes prayer, prayer, and more prayer. As we've seen, there is no magic formula for transforming a struggling church into a successful one. The examples here aren't for you to copy, but to give you encouragement. To the extent that their problems mirror your own, you can certainly borrow from their playbook. The more important step is to assess the unique set of challenges, strengths, and opportunities God has given your church and come up with a plan of action that fits them.

Another point to remember as you renew your church is that God is used to working with imperfect people. No doubt your pathway would be easier if there were remarkably talented church members, or well-connected ones, or generous members with lots of money signing up to help get the job done. That's probably not the team God gave you. Yet He knows who and what you need before you ask.

The Bible tells us many stories of people whose faith got them out of seemingly hopeless situations. Moses and his followers were delivered from their enemies by the parting of the Red Sea; Paul was freed from prison by an earthquake. There's no telling what God might use to revitalize your church. It probably won't be a parting of the nearest river or shaking your old building until it falls down. But it will be, as those historic events were, whatever it takes to solve the problem.

We also see from the Bible that Moses, Paul, and many other followers of Christ accompanied their prayer and faith with plenty of elbow grease. They didn't sit on the railroad track, as the old saying goes, and pray that the train wouldn't come. They used their God-given talents and worked extremely hard, doing all they could to reach their goals, then had faith that God would do what they could not.

Your shrinking church can grow again. The process can start with you, right here, right now. My prayer is that God will use you to renew His church in a mighty way and that your example will in turn be an encouragement to others. I look forward to the day when we'll all enjoy being part of a wonderful new phenomenon: the incredible expanding church. Nothing can stop it!

Notes

1. "In Europe, God Is (Not) Dead," *The Wall Street Journal*, 14 July 2007, A–8.

2. Mac Brunson and Ergun Caner, *Why Churches Die* (Nashville: Broadman & Holman, 2005), 77.

3. Lewis A. Drummond, *Ripe for Harvest* (Nashville: Broadman & Holman, 2001), 157–58.

4. Rick Warren, *The Purpose Driven Church* (Grand Rapids: Zondervan, 1995).

5. David Dockery, gen. ed., *Holman Bible Handbook* (Nashville: Broadman & Holman, 1992).

6. Warren, *The Purpose Driven Church*, 77.

7. Gene Mims, *The Seven Churches Not in the Book of Revelation* (Nashville: Broadman & Holman, 2001).

8. Ibid., 56–58.

9. Thom Rainer and Eric Geiger, *Simple Church* (Nashville: B&H Publishing Group, 2006), chapter 4.

10. Thom Rainer, *Breakout Churches* (Grand Rapids: Zondervan, 2005), 57–58.

11. Warren, *The Purpose Drive Church*, 111.

12. Tom Fitzpatrick, "Advertiser," quoted in *Reader's Digest* (April 1998), 72.

13. Clyde Fant, *Preaching for Today* (San Francisco: Harper San Francisco, 1987).

14. Billy Graham, *Just As I Am* (New York: HarperCollins, 1997), 52–53.

15. *Holman Bible Handbook*, 715–16.

16. Rainer, *Breakout Churches*.

17. Jim Collins, *Good to Great: Why Some Companies Make the Leap . . . and Others Don't* (New York: HarperCollins, 2001).

18. Rainer, *Breakout Churches*, 30.

19. Warren, *The Purpose Driven Church*, 280.

20. Rainer, *Breakout Churches*, 142.

21. Ibid., 91.

22. Ibid.

23. Ibid., 99–100.

24. Ed Stetzer and Mike Dodson, *Comeback Churches* (Nashville: B&H Publishing Group, 2007), 50–52.

25. Gary L. McIntosh, *Biblical Church Growth* (Grand Rapids: Baker Books, 2003), 118–19.

26. Howard Snyder, *Evaluating the Church Growth Movement* (Grand Rapids: Zondervan, 2004), 211–12.

27. Stetzer and Dodson, *Comeback Churches*, 58.

28. Ibid., 7.

29. Ibid., 98.

30. Thom Rainer, *High Expectations: The Remarkable Secret of Keeping People in Your Church* (Nashville: Broadman & Holman, 1999).

31. Stetzer and Dodson, *Comeback Churches*, 126.

32. Rainer, *Breakout Churches*, 221.

33. Ibid., 225.

34. Ibid., 227.

35. Ibid., 232.

36. Ibid., 238.

37. Rick Warren, *The Purpose Driven Life* (Grand Rapids: Zondervan, 2007), 25ff.

38. Rainer and Geiger, *Simple Church*, 8.

39. Ibid., 14.

40. Greg Laurie, *The Upside Down Church* (Wheaton: Tyndale House, 1999), 71.

41. Drummond, *Ripe for Harvest,* 107–9.

42. Stetzer and Dodson, *Comeback Churches,* 78–95.

43. Ibid., 84.

44. Henry Blackaby and Claude King, *Experiencing God* (Nashville: Broadman & Holman, 1994), 269.